EFFECTIVE REMOTE WORKING TECHNIQUES FOR MANAGERS

Nine Ways to Boost Your Productivity While Working Wherever You Like

HARI SINGH

NDP
NEARLY
DONE
PUBLISHING

Copyright © 2020 by Nearly Done Publishing

All rights reserved.

No part of this book may be reproduced in any form or by any electronic or mechanical means, including information storage and retrieval systems, without written permission from the author, except for the use of brief quotations in a book review.

Legal & Disclaimer

The information contained in this book and its contents is not designed to replace or take the place of any form of medical or professional advice; and is not meant to replace the need for independent medical, financial, legal or other professional advice or services, as may be required. The content and information in this book has been provided for educational and entertainment purposes only.

The content and information contained in this book has been compiled from sources deemed reliable, and it is accurate to the best of the Author's knowledge, information and belief. However, the Author cannot guarantee its accuracy and validity and cannot be held liable for any errors and/or omissions. Further, changes are periodically made to this book as and when needed. Where appropriate and/or necessary, you must consult a professional (including but not limited to your doctor, attorney, financial advisor or such other professional advisor) before using any of the suggested remedies, techniques, or information in this book.

Upon using the contents and information contained in this book, you agree to hold harmless the Author from and against any damages, costs, and expenses, including any legal fees potentially resulting from the application of any of the information provided by this book. This disclaimer applies to any loss, damages or injury caused by the use and application, whether directly or indirectly, of any advice or information presented, whether for breach of contract, tort, negligence, personal injury, criminal intent, or under any other cause of action.

You agree to accept all risks of using the information presented inside this book.

You agree that by continuing to read this book, where appropriate and/or necessary, you shall consult a professional (including but not limited to your doctor, attorney, or financial advisor or such other advisor as needed) before using any of the suggested remedies, techniques, or information in this book.

CONTENTS

Introduction	vii
The World Tomorrow	1
Aligning your remote teams goals	9
Create a distraction-free workbase	29
Building productive habits	39
Stay healthy while working remotely	45
Equip your team with tech and productivity tools	57
Boost your teams morale	85
Take time to relax	99
Provide remote socialisation opportunities	123
Final words	129
Resources	131

INTRODUCTION

Whether you are a new remote work manager or an experienced one, you still need to keep yourself updated with the evolution in the modern remote world especially now that many are hopping into the remote work bandwagon either by force or by trend.

Managing remote workers can be a more difficult task than what you expect, especially if you have no previous experience dealing with remote workers.

As much as remote working is full of challenges, there are relatively quick ways that remote managers can do to help ease the transition, including:

- Establishing a regular daily check-in meeting
- Providing appropriate communication technology
- Establishing rules of engagement
- Maintaining and encouraging social interactions
- Giving encouragement and emotional support

So here are some questions you can ask yourself.

- Do you want to explore the possibility of working in a remote environment?
- Are you exploring ways to become more productive even when working in a remote situation while managing other remote workers?
- Are you used to working in a traditional office environment and are now forced to work remotely?

If you think you have been looking for a solution on how to improve your working condition and that of your team, but challenges keep on hindering you from maximising your productivity and performance, then it's time that you turn the pages of this book and find the right solution to your existing problems. We all know there's always a solution to every issue and it's just a matter of finding it in the right place at the right time.

Boosting productivity will keep your mind off the difference in your working environment, and this book will provide you with practical steps on how to set up your environment so that you can have the focus you need to be able to deliver the same level of performance or even beyond that. We will also be teaching you how to deal with the potential pitfalls of working remotely as well as enhancing performance so that you can stop being disturbed by the idea that you are working alone.

The concept of working in a traditional office that is now becoming more outdated and will leave you no choice but to adapt to a new working lifestyle as more and more companies embrace remote working wholly or partially.

I have been a web development specialist contractor for

more than 16 years, and in this time I have witnessed several transitions – from companies insisting that their workers should be working onsite at all times or reluctantly one or two days a week, to fully remote working enforced by powers outside of their control. Through all these years of experience working with clients of differing opinions on what remote operation should be, I have seen many mistakes committed by managers in various senior-level positions and was able to provide the solutions to many issues surrounding their job roles.

As soon as they have applied these techniques they learned from me, they were quickly experiencing an explosion in their productivity. What used to take then eight hours to do in a typical office environment, they were able to achieve only in six hours or even four after they have fully optimised their performance in an improved working environment.

As I have been there before where you are now, let me help you excel in your newly remote situation. I will transform you from being a working newbie to a total powerhouse so completely that your colleagues will be intrigued and will try to discover what you are doing and how they can utilise these techniques for themselves.

I will be teaching you the same solutions through this book for you to achieve the same productivity they got so you can maximise productivity and have more time left for yourself and your family. Regardless of where you are working, there should always be a balance in life and work.

From here, I will be taking you from a hardcore office worker to become a hardcore remote worker while using these simple techniques in place. As a bonus, you will become stronger both mentally and physically and end up having more time on your hands with which you know what to do.

By ensuring that my tools and processes were in place, I experienced zero downtime when forced to make the wholesale switch recently, and I was up and running faster than anyone else in my team who were then also relying on my experience to get them up and running too. Moving into this current enforced situation was seamless for me and seemed to be just another typical working day – no stress, no fuss!

If you are willing to learn the techniques contained in this book and make real changes, then every chapter will build you into an effective manager in this remote situation. Remember that TIME is of the essence and productivity relies on quality time.

The real power, however, comes when you combine these techniques and their effects to boost your productivity so much that your colleagues will start asking you for tips as they start feeling that they are being left behind!

Furthermore, NOW is the time for you to set up good habits before detrimental ones bed in to your daily routine. Start reading this book and start enjoying a more productive life while working remotely.

THE WORLD TOMORROW

Now, with the continuing development in technology and digital transformation in businesses, the increasing number of remote workers is getting becoming more evident. **Intuit** – a leading American business and financial software company developing and selling financial, accounting, and tax preparation software and related services, recently reported that:

- Contingent workers will make up about 40% of the workforce by 2020
- Traditional full-time jobs with full benefits will be harder to find
- Small business will be establishing their collaborative networks of contingent workers resulting in increasing numbers of self-employment, personal, as well as micro-businesses.

There is going to be a bright future for remote workers, nd there will be more positions open for remote managers.

The popularity of working remotely has risen over these past few years as many people find it more exciting to work in a detached setting. Working remotely has its many benefits, but like any other job, it also involves many challenges.

For one, remote work can be very demanding and challenging, especially for those who are still starting. You will find yourself prone to suffering from loneliness, distraction, and procrastination. While the benefits and comfort of working anywhere are immense, the challenges which you are facing as a remote worker may lead to many issues including the lack of work-life balance and it is even tougher for remote managers who will be managing remote workers with diverse cultures across multiple time zones.

Although it is preferable to establish clear remote-work policies and training in advance, there are times, especially in a crisis or other fast-changing circumstances that this level of preparation is not feasible. However, there are some specific research-based steps that you, as a remote manager, can learn and put into action without much effort to improve the engagement and productivity of remote workers who also may have had little time to prepare.

It is therefore crucial for managers to understand the different factors that make remote work especially demanding. If not, even high-performing employees may experience a decline in their job performances and engagement once they start working in an isolated fashion, especially in the absence of training and preparation.

When working in social isolation, loneliness can be one of the most common complaints among remote workers who are missing the opportunities of informal social interactions that an office setting offers to those with a more extraverted personality. They may suffer more from isolation in the short-run, especially when there's a lack of opportunities to connect with others in their remote work environment. However, a longer time-span of separation can cause any employee to feel less belonging to their organisational structure, and this may lead to an increased intention to leave.

THE CHALLENGES OF MANAGING A TEAM OF REMOTE WORKERS

While there are numerous advantages for hiring remote workers, there are also some definite drawbacks for doing so. The issue revolves around the fact that most managers are still not familiar with the challenges of, and specialised skills required to, manage remote workers.

Remote work is not like the typical work structure, and while there may be some significant benefits, there are also unique and unanticipated challenges both in hiring and managing remote workers.

Buffer's State of Remote Work stated the major challenges of remote work (Buffer, n.d.). In 2018, there was this neuroscience report which revealed that when mice are put in isolation and away from their typical social structure, their brain cells showed signs of social interaction atrophy which means that parts of their brain started dying when they were separated from other mice. Isolation and loneliness in humans are just as detrimental as those in mice. Lengthened isolation can lead to anxiety and depression in extreme cases. Being a manager of remote workers, it is imperative that you are aware of this. It is your responsibility to engage them socially with the rest of the team whenever possible.

Loneliness and Social Isolation

It can be easy to take for granted or neglect the necessity of regular human interaction until you find yourself thrown into a situation where you have to manage a set of workers you don't personally know or seen in person.

Humans, by nature, are sociable animals, so it won't be surprising that being isolated at home can have a considerable impact not only on our mental health but also on our physical health.

Communication Issues

The sense of being left out, let's say when giving an opinion is more likely to happen in a remote work setting than in a shared physical workplace. Because remote workers vary individually in personality, beliefs, culture, and in many other things, there may be some remote workers under you who felt that they aren't given any attention nor did you take notice of the way they're working. A survey of remote workers conducted by Indeed disclosed that about 37 per cent of the participants believed that working remotely can lead to reduced visibility and less opportunity for the company's leadership (Indeed, 2018).

Lack of Access to Information

It is sometimes surprising how long it is before a fellow remote worker can provide you with information on something or when you are just asking about anything. Even a simple reply to a question can become a significant obstacle to a home-based worker.

This kind of situational issue can extend beyond task-related work to interpersonal challenges that can happen among remote team members. It is because of the lack of mutual knowledge translates to a lack of understanding or giving co-workers the benefit of the doubt when you do not know about what is happening on the other side.

With all these challenges, building trust and rapport with your remote workers can counter them. Getting to know each other while having regular and dedicated check-ins weekly will help create a strong bond within the remote team.

BUILDING A HIGH PERFORMANCE REMOTE TEAM

A high performance remote team is like an elite combat unit in a military organisation. They have a specific goal and move as one just to achieve it. They collaborate, resolve, innovate, and strive to produce superior results.

A superior remote team is an asset in all forms or organisations, which is not surprising why every corporate business aims to have this kind of remote team in their organisation. It takes deliberate action along with meticulous planning plus great leadership and business culture for an organisation to nurture and grow high performance remote teams.

Clarity of Vision and Goals

Any team can work best when they have a clear and definite vision and goal to guide them. For high performance teams, this is doubly important, and the team manager needs to ensure that the vision and goals are always on top of each tea member's list of priorities.

When at work, it is common for workers to lose sight of the targets, and one way the remote manager can do to help them is to break down the goal into smaller tasks or objectives. Once the team achieves its objectives, you inform the whole team and update them on the overall performance and progress.

It is not enough for the team to know their goal. Each team member must be able to relate their contributions—to the achievement or realisation of the overall goal. And to develop unity and bonding within the team, the remote team manager needs to show how individual roles feed into and support the functions of other team members. Recognising what one has contributed to the overall performance and progress of the whole team can considerably drive each team member to do their best.

As the manager of the team, you can not only lead your team in setting your goal but can also stretch goals—those that are more challenging to realise. If the team failed to achieve the objective for some reason, it must not be viewed negatively but will be used to build the morale of the team, knowing that they have done their part in tackling something challenging.

MAKE EVERYTHING EXPLICIT

The office of a non-remote worker inherently comes with many boundaries. They need to commute to a specific workplace, arrive and leave at a particular time. Everything is according to schedule – breaks, meetings, events and other parts of the day. These boundaries come naturally and are a part of the whole working process – easily understood and accepted. While they are significant to the entire structure, none of them exists in a remote team, hence; you need to make them explicit.

What is vital in running a remote team is to have a one-page document that defined the most important rules and processes – how they make decisions, and each of the team members must have a copy of that, read it at least once a week to make sure that everyone is on the same page while at work.

What is significant here is not the fact that you need a one-page document of all the rules and processes, but that through it, you are explicitly setting boundaries that every member of the remote team must acccpt and respect. However, these boundaries aren't set in stone, for you can always realign any part if the need arises.

These explicit rules and processes constitute a general guideline that helps in particular, when onboarding a remote employee. Without an exact method, it can be frustrating for everyone – the new employee and you who manages the team. Processes vary between remote companies, and they can also change later. However, you'll soon find out that the most successful ones are those remote teams with their guidelines explicitly documents and accessible to everyone in the group.

ALIGNING YOUR REMOTE TEAMS GOALS

The world is continually changing, and so is the way people are working. When there are not many options left but bring your work home, you have to find ways to adjust your lifestyle. Technology has evolved too in a way that you don't feel the necessity of being in your standard office space just to accomplish all your assigned tasks and responsibilities.

Such changes in your work styles and technology affect the way you manage people under your supervision when you work with a team. As a remote leader, you need to fine-tune yourself in a way that your team or your employees remain productive even when out of sight and reach goals successfully while accomodating flexible working styles. What can make this up and come is a certain amount of trust plus intentional communication.

Given that there is a proper goal to guide everyone in your team, the whole process can work seamlessly. Setting clear goals which involve specific parameters allows regular check-ins and evaluations which can help a manager lead remote teams efficiently and effectively.

When setting goals, there are certain things you need to bear in mind.

The End-Result

When setting your goal, the first thing you need to consider is the key result. Brainstorm with your remote team members to be able to determine your personal and professional goals. As the team manager, you need to outline the team goals – both short and long term. Remember that even when all of you are working separately, with the right technology, you can still manage to conduct your brainstorming activities.

When all are focusing on the outcome, all will know what to deliver, and you will be at peace knowing that everyone in your team is working towards a common tangible goal to help the organisation grow.

SET SMARTER GOALS

To make sure that the goals you are setting are clear and achievable, you must stick to certain specifications.

S – Specific
M – Measurable
A – Attainable
R – Relevant
T – Time-bound
E – Evaluated
R – Reviewed

To frame SMARTER goals, let us now understand what

it is to set SMARTER GOALS.

SPECIFIC

Goals that answer to the 5Ws are more accurate.

- **What** do you intend to achieve?
- **Why** is it essential to achieve this goal?
- **Who** are will help you to achieve this goal?
- **When** are you going to achieve this goal?
- **Where** are the resources you could use in achieving your goal? Include limitations as well.

MEASURABLE

It will be easy for you to track down your progress when the goal is measurable. Gauging progress would help remote workers to stay in tune and motivated for every step makes them feel that they are getting nearer to their target.

ACHIEVABLE

Setting the goal to be achievable stretches the team's potential for success. So when setting targets with your team, make sure that you realise the difference between realistic goals and those that aren't.

RELEVANT

Make sure that you understand the dependencies of the goal since the right timing counts for the success of the whole team. So ask yourself this - Should we prioritise this? Is this the right time for doing this? Your task would be a lot easier if you know the answers to these questions.

TIME-BOUND

A goal needs to have a specific deadline, or your team members will not be motivated to work towards its achievement. Indefinite goals tend to give one the feeling that you can achieve it anytime and therefore, you tend to neglect it. Even when it is a long-term one, it is vital to give it a target date.

REVIEW

When you have set the goals for your remote team, note that it is not yet the end of them. Tracking progress at regular intervals will prevent you and your team from getting off track, and you can quickly realign some policies or make some adjustments when once you see that something is off. Most of the time, the reality is different from our ideas and by tracking your team's progress will allow you to take the right measures when something goes wrong straight away. Take note that nothing is wrong with changing tack on your way to completing your goals; however, for you to understand what is happening, you need to review your goals often.

Alternatively, there is available goal-setting software that would ease out the goal-setting process and can help your team create, track, and analyse goals in real-time. An example is the Objectives and Key Results (OKRS) - a collaborative goal-setting tool for the use of individuals and teams to help them set challenging and ambitious goals.

THINGS TO REMEMBER WHEN SETTING GOALS

Achieving your business goals generally requires setting measurable goals so you can monitor your progress, keep track of your team member's contributions, and eventually see if you can reach your objectives. Objectives are those short-term steps you need to do in support of your goal.

Let us learn these business tactics that some successful remote managers are using to set measurable goals with their remote teams to achieve the outcome they are expecting for business growth and development.

Identify Goals that are Measurable with Metrics

When much of the work in a remote business is done online, many decision made are data-driven – that is, there are many opportunities to create quantifiable goals.

With remote team members, tying up goals to specific and quantitative objectives makes things clear for them to know what is required of them to achieve a satisfactory outcome.

Regardless of the goal you are setting, establishing a concrete metric will provide your team members with a clear direction and put them on the path for success.

Break Goals into Smaller Tasks

It will be easier for you to manage and measure your business goal if you break them into smaller tasks or objectives. These smaller segments are also referred to as Key Performance Indicators (KPIs) – a set of defined and measurable outcomes that can be tracked and can indicate that you are on the right way to achieving your goal. With these indicators, you as the manager of the team will be able to see more clearly if the goal is on time or if team members are struggling to meet the deadline or if it better to reevaluate your goal.

Schedule Enough Time for the Goal to Complete

You may have good intentions when determining how much time you need to accomplish a given task; however, we have this tendency to be too optimistic in the estimation of time and resources. When planning with your team, make sure that you allocate extra time, a percentage buffer to account for last-minute changes and other things that may go beyond your control like a sick team member, or an accident.

With this buffer, you have less stress, and it makes the goal more attainable, especially when you have multiple teams working together in different locations.

Review Goal Regularly for Possible Adjustments

Reviewing the progress of individual team members along with the overall team is the key to staying on track and to determining if the individuals' performance is on a trajectory towards timely completion. While business development goals usually go through multiple phases before completion, reviewing with your team on a weekly, monthly, and quarterly basis are essential to keeping everyone on track while ensuring that small tasks are completed, and communication within the team remains open.

To measure progress consistently, establish a schedule for

review meetings during the initial goal-planning stage. This review will keep team members accountable and focused while working steadily towards the completion date and metrics.

Achieving business development and growth goals, either an individual or with your team, cultivates a workplace culture of clear communication, job satisfaction, and greater motivation towards the completion of future goals – which is sure to set success for your business.

PRACTICAL WAYS TO BUILD AND GROW A POSITIVE BUSINESS CULTURE WITH A REMOTE TEAM

Due to modern technology, there is a massive shift occurring in the global work environment, and such changes are accelerating more quickly than ever before.

Gone are the days of centralised organisations, as tasks and responsibilities are now decentralised and distributed to remote teams. Now, remote team working are becoming more popularised as people from different locations – whether they are just across the street or on the other side of the world – are working together in a team.

So if you happen to manage a remote team, how can you create an environment of positive behaviour and continue to grow a positive business culture with your team.

Understanding the Value of Remote Working

Many studies proved that remote working indeed had valuable effects on workers' happiness, productivity, and general well-being. Harvard Business Review tackled an experiment involving a Chinese call centre where workers were provided with the opportunity to work at home for about nine months. About 50% of the participants were allowed to telecommute while the rest remain working in the office. When performances of the two groups were compared at the end of the nine months, the result showed that those working at home weren't only happier and less likely to quit, but were even more productive than those who were left working in the office (Bloom, 2014). Some studies likewise proved that it is not only workers who derived benefits from working at home; companies can benefit from adopting the new remote work setting (Analytics, 2016).

Some of the key benefits are:

- Improved employees satisfaction
- Increased productivity
- Reduces unscheduled absences
- Saves corporate cost
- Increases collaboration
- Cuts down on wasteful meetings
- Expands talent pool

As one can see, there are myriads of benefits available for both employers and workers when using remote teams as an option.

Once you have assembled a fantastic team of talented and skilful people and yet for some reason, the culture within your business organisation is not heading to the direction you want it to go, then maybe, you should take a moment to stop and reflect on what is essential for your business. Do you have a set of existing corporate values against which you can measure yourselves?

Without strong leadership and clear direction, a company may keep plodding along; however, the lack of unity and direction will eventually take its toll on business productivity and revenues.

Imagine a sports team where everyone gets on board fully motivated, but because there is no clear direction, they are losing more games than winning. Soon enough, you will observe that everyone starts showing signs of disagreement.

Refining Corporate Values

The company values serve as the core of positive business culture. Without instilling a set of values to measure your business organisation against, can be an enormous waste of time, money, and energy. Corporate values have the power to make a significant improvement in your business culture.

Many businesses tend to concentrate on the products and services they are providing while neglecting the needs of their workers and employees, which is why the businesses suffer in the long run. After all, it is the morale – working behaviour of the employees and workers towards the company that creates the business culture. To be able to provide your clients and customers with excellent products and services, you need to go back to the basics – that is, creating a positive business or company culture. Having a clear set of values can harness the direction of your corporate culture.

Determine Business Values as a Team

Corporate values are not static and should be reviewed

from time to time. Brainstorm values and goals as a team to get buy-in, for when the corporate values are determined as a team, it gets every team member inspired for the long term. They would be motivated to head back to work every morning instead of dragging themselves from their beds. Note that everyone is motivated when it is their values and goals they are trying to realise.

Give Way to Positive Communication

Positive communication is not about those random chats during coffee breaks but focusing on positive messages that can help encourage everyone to contribute to a positive culture.

Communication is essential to living, and employers have to find ways to effectively communicate with subordinates to build a supportive relationship that is most required, especially during challenging situations.

Listen to Team Members' Feedback

It is essential to listen to feedback coming from employees to know where improvement is needed. Listening to feedback and taking actions to show that you are interested to know value employees' opinions and suggestions while doing whatever is required to improve.

A constructive opinion or suggestion is useful as it assists the employer to understand better areas that are lacking and in need of improvement. There is nothing that can't be changed or adjusted when needed for the development and performance of the business. Be it in the form of an employees' survey or performance review; it is for the betterment of the workplace to listen to team members to help them become more effective than they are now.

Show Care and Concern

Everyone wants to feel appreciated when they work on something, which is why they spend more time on work than spending time with themselves, family, or loved ones. When remote team managers show concern for their team members, it means that they are not only concerned in increasing the business revenues or profit, but they are also expressing their care for the team as well as for each team member. When the manager cares, the members likewise return the favour by doing their best.

Knowing Their Roles

Creating a positive business culture includes identifying the individual roles of each team member and assisting them to be better at it or helping them learn new skills. When they succeed, it's for your benefit, too.

Welcome New Ideas

When you encourage your teammates to share their ideas, opinions, or suggestion through brainstorming activities, they will realise that their views are significant to them as well as to the company. This recognition will allow them to grow and get more creative.

Develop a supportive business climate that nurtures personal and professional growth.

. . .

Be Rewarding

Your team members deserve the best when they help achieve the company's goal through their best performance. So make sure to give credit when and to whom it is due even when it just through a message of appreciation. Awarding them will small tokens, vouchers, gift certificates, or cash incentives for the best remote team member of the month will motivate other members to do better in the future.

Adopt Flexibility

Although you have set rules and guidelines to follow, you will soon see that some won't be applicable at all times. There will always be exemptions to these rules.

Once workers are allowed to be flexible, they tend to be more dedicated and committed to their jobs. When you give them more autonomy to explore different methods, it allows their mind to be more innovative and creative in their ideas and in providing a solution to an issue.

Entertain Humour

We can't be serious at all ties. Stress is just around the corner, and if we add a little fun and humour to a stressful work environment, your team members will feel a bit relaxed and may complete the task earlier than expected. By adding humour at work with a positive attitude, there will be more productivity. Remember that laughter is the best medicine, and an ounce of it can drive stress away.

A company need not neglect its moral obligation to its workers in the pursuit of success. One has to look after their welfare and well-being to create a positive culture.

Employees today, especially those belonging to the millennial generation down, expect to work in a company which talks, not only of benefits and paychecks. They are more concerned with their emotional satisfaction for they want to feel needed and useful in the company while they want to have a little fun, given how many hours they spend on their job in a week. If you want to create a positive business culture, you better give your teammates a reason to look forward to work every day.

COMMUNICATING YOUR CULTURE

While you may speak of your corporate values, company culture must be expressed at the same level of importance.

Make the document clear, well written, and inspiring. Having, team members that are apart, this document becomes even more critical. It must be able to articulate the company's culture to everyone clearly – both new and old members, right from the start. The document should be clear about how performance will be gauged, what will be expected of team members, and how you assess team members for cultural fit.

You should regularly review the documented company culture as the business grows and adapt to changes. Let this document be accessible for everyone to read and don't shelve it. Continue to monitor your culture and values to develop a positive company culture.

ENCOURAGE AN ENVIRONMENT OF OPEN COMMUNICATION AND FEEDBACK

You can promote transparency by keeping your communication channels clear and open. With this, you will be encouraging an environment where all team members can contribute and not just those loud extroverts in the team.

Reduce formality associated with communication to drive employees to openly talk and not just stay quiet. For small to average sized teams, being more casual and laid-back with team communications channels are typically better as they become more open and transparent.

SET EXPECTATIONS ON COMMUNICATION METHODS

To help set the tone and encourage communication, set expectations on which channels will be utilised for what topics. To illustrate, let's say that for legal and official documents, always course them through email or cloud file server while casual discussions among team members can take place through Slack or Skype.

By creating a simple guide, you can reduce confusion in communication like what to post and where to post, ensuring everyone has the same idea as you do. So if your existing remote team is using Slack for text discussion and Dropbox for file sharing, make sure to let new team members know about this, so they don't need to inquire from the team just to find out what particular tools are required for specific circumstances.

Encourage your team to leave their communication tools open while at work – either as browser tab or desktop app with notification to keep you instantly updated. Anything as simple as this will keep the communication channel open, thereby creating a more cohesive workplace conducive to collaboration.

TAKE TIME TO KNOW EVERYONE

Knowing your team beyond how they let you know about them is quite challenging, however, make it a point to learn more about them through informal or casual discussions.

You could make this a game. Simple and fun activities like this can help grow a positive business culture within a remote team.

COMMUNICATE MORE!

Your remote team culture will either flourish or fail because of communication. Get it wrong, and you'll see that you won't be able to create a positive business culture. Better set aside regular times for all-hands chatting when possible. If the difference in time zones will be an issue, set up two meetings in differing zones. Cover what the group works on, discuss details on any decisions affecting the team, and emphasise that you need open communication and feedback. These will help share updates and encourage the entire team.

Set policy regarding the use of chat software – like they can send messages even when you're not around so that once you get back to work mode, you can read it. However, make sure not to allow team members to work around the clock. Practices like this can breed contempt and workers are sure to burnout and would no longer be productive and effective at work.

Conduct annual or quarterly face-to-face meetings using video conferencing, allowing team members to recognise their teammates, read reactions, and facial expressions which can someone establish familiarity and bonding as time moves on. Body language and other nonverbal communications help one learn more about someone as they observe their body movements while listening to what they are saying.

MEASURE YOUR REMOTE TEAM ENGAGEMENT

Setting a monthly or quarterly pulse survey can help you measure your remote team members' sentiments. Just don't focus on work-related issues or topics but also consider asking them about general happiness and mood to encourage openness among the team, which can help alleviate any sense of isolation or lack of communication.

TIPS TO HELP YOUR TEAM WORK IN ALIGNMENT WITH THE BUSINESS GOAL

Now that about 52 per cent of the global workforce is working remotely (Simovic, 2020), it is becoming essential for businesses to cultivate productive and engaging remote teams. The key factor is the alignment of these team members with the company goals.

Studies revealed that productivity increases by at least 56 per cent when employees understand how their work contributes to company goals and objectives (Gallup, Inc., 2019).

Here are some tips on how you can help your remote teamwork in alignment with the business or company goal.

COMMUNICATE REGULARLY

Without excellent communication, remote teams can't work efficiently and effectively. It is therefore crucial in any remote group dynamic with limited interaction to use explicit platforms like email and instant messaging even more.

You may schedule a regular teleconferencing or group chats to provide plenty of opportunities for information sharing. Short and focused daily check-ins are a great way to keep every team member aware of what the others are doing and sense the bigger picture.

You may also create a digital office space using Slack when you can instantly "pop over" for a quick chat. Schedule open-ended brainstorming sessions where your team can come together and create whiteboard ideas digitally. This will help focus and strength the company's collective vision. With clear and frequent communication, everyone can keep company's goal top in mind while fostering a sense of close connections among team members.

CULTIVATE INTER-PERSONAL CONNECTIONS

Cultivating closeness among members of the team who haven't personally seen each other is one of the biggest challenges for remote team managers. With the absence of a shared space for office work, there can be less opportunity for impromptu conversations. Although, you may schedule some days when the team can have online discussions focusing on daily tasks and responsibilities, creating a more personal dynamic within a distributed organisation can significantly increase connectedness. It can likewise motivate them to contribute to the company's vision instead of just completing jobs in isolation. Workers and employees are more productive with active engagement which leads to less turnover and therefore more revenues for the company.

To cultivate a sense of community among remote team members, try creating spaces to get more personal. Have a Slack chat to have fun conversations as well as designate time during check-ins to discuss personal well-being. You may likewise require all meetings to be via video calls so they can be more focused, intimate, and engaging.

The more opportunities there are for your team to have bonding moments on an interpersonal level, the closer they will get and the more motivated they will be to perform their best. Note that a worker works best when happy.

MANAGE CONFLICT EFFECTIVELY

Whether you are managing a remote team of workers in a shared office, dealing with disputes can be a particularly difficult task to accomplish. However, it even more magnified when relationships and interactions are limited to the digital sphere. Cultivating a team that connects well builds trust, which makes conflicts easier to handle. With a better environment and good intentions, workers and teammates can avoid feeling isolated and resentment towards fellow remote workers.

Just like in any other managing roles, it is vital to allow your team members to join in goal-setting discussions so they can also provide positive and negative feedback.

Fostering a sense of trust among team members and handling disagreements with fair judgment, you are bringing the team together while developing in them a collective mindset that works toward shared company goals.

CREATE GOAL-CENTRED TASKS

Because you are in charge of managing the whole team of remote workers, you have to make sure that everything is tied up to the big picture. For example, opening and closing check-in meetings by drawing connections to overarching goals can keep team members on the same page with you. Don't forget to continually remind them that their actions contribute to company goals for it gives meaning to their daily tasks and makes them feel that they are a part of the whole company to which they belong. This sense of belonging drives them to do more for the goodness of the entire team and company.

HAVE CLEAR AND DEFINITE EXPECTATIONS

For a better understanding of how work contributes to the big picture, it is crucial to have a transparent system for tracking and planning. It is by providing crystal clear instructions and setting definite expectations that these remote team members can reserve their energy for productivity instead of figuring out what needs to be done.

With particularly designated channels assigned for different types of tasks and messages, team members will be more alert as information is more relevant. It can keep them on track, and you can help them judge their productivity by themselves by setting individual or team goals with measurable results.

Remote work is flexible by nature that imposing structure through routines can be helpful and creates a culture of reliability. Once you can communicate clearly, it will be much easier for employees to achieve smaller goals that will contribute to the big and long term goal.

REMAIN TRANSPARENT

Once remote workers have a clear understanding of what they are doing and why they are doing it, expect their performance level to rise, and the quality of deliverables to improve when they are working not only for the sake of earning their salary. They will likewise prioritise their tasks more effectively and take ownership of their work. By creating a culture of transparency and giving them the chance to hear the reasons behind every decision you are making and how they relate to the bigger goal, you are making them feel that they are an integral part of the bigger picture. With shared communication channels, processes, and decisions get more visible to everyone. It is by sharing information that you can help your team see how things connect within the team structure and how their work is crucial to the overall business plan. Accomplishing individual tasks, therefore, proves vital to achieving the end goal.

Whether you have been managing a remote team for quite some time or you are just starting, learning how to keep team goals aligned regardless of the distance in location will be a significant factor in the success of business in the future.

CREATE A DISTRACTION-FREE WORKBASE

Since the beginning of 2020, more than 85% of organisations in the United States have encouraged employees to work from home. These workers have experienced juggling work and home activities daily. Just imagine the workplace filled with the commotion coming from the children or a pet. How do you cope up with this situation and stay laser-focused?

We, humans, are known for being resilient and adaptable —this is our strength. Adjusting to a new working environment may be challenging but not altogether impossible. This chapter will talk about distractions and some techniques on how you, as a remote manager, can generate a distraction-free workplace.

HOW DO DISTRACTIONS AFFECT PRODUCTIVITY?

One of the most significant issues with distractions in the workplace is that they directly lead to productivity loss which is tied to the number of hours employees and workers lose due to their lack of focus on their tasks. American businesses are losing as much as $650 billion per year due to workplace distractions (Kuligowski, 2019).

Conversely, workers likewise recognise the detrimental impact of distraction on productivity. A Udemy report into the effects of workplace distractions on employees (Toluna Group, 2018) shows that:

- 20% believe that they are aren't able to reach their full potential and career advancement
- 50% believe that they are significantly less productive
- 54% believe they aren't performing as they should

A study made by researchers from Simon Fraser University revealed that how one is affected by distractions is dependent on their working memory capacity (Neuroscience News, 2016).

Better memory equates to higher ability to avoid distractions

---

Those who are performing well in memory tasks (indicating high working memory capacity) are proven more efficient in combating distractions.

Poor memory equates to lower ability to avoid distractions

Those who are performing poorly in memory tasks (indicating low memory capacity) are proven to fail in surpassing distractions quickly.

Now that we have established the impact of distractions on productivity, a remote team manager needs to help team members resolve issues in their respective workplaces. Here are some tips on how to handle work-related distractions to help your team be less distracted and more focused on their tasks.

Introduce No-Meeting Days

Remember that distraction is common in remote work, and distractions that come from managers are not exempted. Udemy survey stated that twenty three per cent of respondents proposed introducing a no-meeting day in a week to avoid distractions and interruptions from work.

Limit the Time Remote Team Spends on Meeting

Communication is essential, but if you can limit each meeting to 15-20 minutes and still be able to cover crucial points, the better, so your team can be more productive with their time. You can keep track of the time spent on meetings to make sure that everyone sticks to the limit, which brings us the next item.

Set a Clear Agenda for Each Meeting

Time is important for each remote team worker, so make

sure that you don't waste a single minute. Each scheduled meeting is meant to be productive and should have a clear and concise agenda to cover. Sending prior notice about an upcoming schedule will familiarise the team, and everyone will think about concerns and questions to ask related to the matter during the meeting.

Also, make sure to invite only those who have direct concern over the agenda lest it can be a waste of time for participants if topics tackled in the meeting are not relevant. It would be more productive for the entire team or company if they are working instead of wasting their time listening when the matter does not directly involve them. You could send them an extract from the minutes of the meeting later to notify them of any action taken for the sake of updating the whole team if needed.

As a remote manager, you must be concerned with your productivity as well as that of your team, so you must likewise create a distraction-free zone in the comfort of your home.

Here are ways for you to do it so you can work effectively, efficiently, and productively.

DESIGNATE YOUR WORK AREA

Whether it is your desk, room, or basement, you should create a separate space that you can use as your workspace. It should be an area you can immediately associate with work and disconnect from the rest of your home.

Most people find it hard to focus on anything when there are over-stimulating elements and environments around them. In a typical office setting, we can get into the working mode right away. It is because the people around us are working hard. In contrast, we can be easily distracted when we hear children's giggles or when our pet acts cute.

Experts found that a typical office worker takes an average of 25 minutes to return to the original task after an interruption. If you are in a more comfortable environment like your home, then the number inevitably increases.

Many people strive to find space in their homes where they can concentrate. Unfortunately, this may serve as a severe challenge to those people who have roommates or family members occupying the same space as theirs. To gain some quietude to your working time, you have to bring order by eliminating the clutter.

As a remote manager, the challenge is doubled. You have to concentrate on managing your work as well as those of other people working under you but are physically far from you.

Let us provide some tips on how to set up your work area:

- Ideally, you should use a room separate from shared spaces. However, if you cannot get a distinct area, try to find a niche space away from the rest of the household's way as much as possible.
- Find a comfortable workspace, including a chair and a proper desk that can hold computer equipment.
- Sit by the window or at least obtain a plant and a good lamp. Feel free to hang up a picture of nature since people tend to be more productive in bright, lush environments.

- Create a music playlist that helps you increase your focus.
- Designate time for screen breaks and lunchtime.
- Get rid of the clutter from your desk and workspace regularly.

Creating a sharp boundary between your work and personal life helps you retain focus. After all, being a remote manager, you will need a quiet space to make video conferences, organise things for your staff, and be productive.

AVOID PHYSICAL AND MENTAL CLUTTER

No one else is going to see how messy or organised your desk is—no one but you.

Clutter negatively affects your life. It can hamper your way with things, especially your productivity in the workplace. A cluttered desk or table lowers productivity level and can negatively affect your mood and resilience. It also creates emotional and mental distress, making you feel like you have no control over your space or life.

Your ability to focus and concentrate can become restricted in cluttered environments. As a result, your brain's ability to process information can be substantially affected. Clutter distracts you, so you are unable to think and accomplish work. It competes for your attention and makes you feel frustrated. Of course, frustrated managers will only achieve inferior results.

Clutter is not merely physical but can be digital as well. It merely means that your computer, smartphone, tablet, and other gadgets are a potential source of clutter. Notifications, files, emails, or anything that competes for your attention are all mere clutter when they are disorganised. Keep in mind that your work computer must be functional and easy to use. How can you manage effectively if you cannot organise things yourself? When your brain has to deal with so many issues, it splits its power and thereby results in inadequate performance and wasted time.

Here are some practical tips that will help you eliminate physical and mental clutters:

Create and Organise a To-Do List

A to-do list is crucial for any remote manager. It should be an actual list and not just a mental one. Good thing that technology allows us to create and organise our tasks through various apps or software. Don't worry; we will talk about these tools later, but good old fashioned pen and paper will do just fine too.

To-do lists help us consolidate scattered ideas, thoughts, and tasks. By identifying what needs doing, you can prioritise critical tasks first, particularly those that occupy the worry space in your mind.

Clean Up Any Actual Clutter

Just as mentioned, physical clutter robs us of clarity. Tidying up will improve not only the visual aspect of our space but also our mental coherence.

Being Mindful Brings Quality Results

Be mindful of all your tasks and activities. When you are working, try to keep your mind there and not with your children, lover, or the upcoming episode of your favourite TV series. Mindfulness encourages a clear mind that can focus and bring productive results. Mindfulness meditation dramatically helps in promoting work productivity.

Set Boundaries

Setting boundaries is not all about the workspace. It may mean telling your children or roommate not to invade your space during working hours. This is also applicable during virtual meetings and discussions by sticking to the topic only and disregarding idle talk.

Prevent Distractions

Many elements around us serve as distractions. If you are working at home, chances are you have many more distractions to deal with. It may be your lovely family, your adorable pet, or the picturesque scenery you see by your window. However, you can follow these simple preventative steps to help you stay focused on your role as a remote manager:

Set Guidelines

Set limits for your cohabitants and yourself, distinctly stating the times when your space is off-limits and the times when interruptions are permissible.

Invest In Headphones

Feel free to use headphones to prevent people from interrupting you. You can also listen to music or sounds that help with your concentration. I highly recommend finding a pair that have noise cancelling to push away distractions.

Avoid Multitasking

No matter how overloaded your to-do list may be, do not multitask. Error rate increases to about 50%, and it would take you twice as long to accomplish your tasks when you try to switch from one task to another in just a short time.

Block Distracting Websites or Apps

Some apps like Facebook Messenger have the option to mute a conversation for an indefinite time or a few hours. You can also put your phone on airplane mode or silent mode. Meanwhile, apps like Focus Me help block social media sites during the work hours, making it easier for you to stay focused and more productive.

Take a Moment to Relax

Nobody can work for eight hours straight without taking a break. Without taking a break, you will find yourself exhausted, which in turn will hurt your productivity. On the other hand, planned breaks improve focus and productivity. Designating specific relaxation times helps you reduce your anxiety levels.

To keep your mind sharp during work, take a break once in a while. Take this opportunity to declutter your workspace, grab a healthy snack, drink water, doing stretching exercises, or take a power nap. Anything is fine as long as it does not go beyond your planned time allocation.

Lunchtime is also an excellent opportunity to change the scenery, even if it is limited to going to the kitchen. Absolutely do not eat lunch at your desk. As much as possible, avoid fiddling your smartphone or tablet while on a break.

BUILDING PRODUCTIVE HABITS

In the world of rapidly changing business nowadays, wearing suits that conform to the office style of work is becoming obsolete. Due to digital communication platforms and HR software, most are taking advantage of the flexibility of this new work and are setting up their own offices at home. According to smallbusiness.co.uk, about half of the workforce will be working remotely from now on. A poll conducted by the website recently revealed that more than half of people who work from home are happier compared to those who work inside an office setting. Factors that lead to this result are not having to commute and wait for long hours to get into the office, no more standard stuffy suits, and, most of all, no ugly office politics.

The truth is, however, the reality isn't always great for those who work from home. While it may be no longer required to commute to get into your workplace, it can be challenging to separate work time and playtime. There are also no more tea or coffee breaks or office politics, but working alone could eventually get boring and lonely, with no one to discuss the latest news, gossips, and fashion trends with you, it will also be easy to forget that you may have been wearing the same clothes that you wore the day before yesterday. However, it doesn't mean that you should give up on doing home business. Instead of quitting, dressing right while working from home can do the trick.

DRESS FOR SUCCESS IN YOUR HOME OFFICE

Before, donning a suit, heading to the office, and working from Monday to Friday were considered the norm. During weekends, on the other hand, wearing casual attire, staying away from the office, and spending your leisure time doing whatever you want is common. To those who work from home, however, this regular routine is abolished one way or another. Since you both work and live at home, the boundary that separates the two can become blurred. So instead of working from Monday to Friday and resting during the weekends, the chances are that you're going to work seven days a week, which could eventually get problematic. You will always risk yourself being in work mode, no matter what time of day it is.

SEPARATING YOUR WORK-LIFE FROM HOME LIFE

Doing the reverse is also risky. While at home, you can easily forgo unfinished work to binge-watch the TV series that you never watched because work got in the way, or spending more time procrastinating on social media. If you don't set clear boundaries, you will eventually find yourself burned out, or sacrificing everything you worked hard for just because you did not do your work.

Even though it's just a simple concept, the clothes you wear can have a massive impact on your mindset as well as your work performance. A fashion psychologist at Hertfordshire University explained that clothing has a symbolic meaning to each one of us. So whenever we put on professional work attire while at work, we are priming our brain to behave in ways consistent to that attire. This act makes you focus and perform more efficiently while at work. The same rule also applies to casual attire; wearing those during weekends will help you relax more.

DRESSING TO IMPRESS

Work relationships aren't always easy, especially when office politics get ugly. Working from home may let you get away from this mess, but there will always be times that it will leave you feeling lonely and isolated. Even if you regularly put smiley emojis on Skype or Facebook, it will never match up to the real thing. Having other people around you while working helps you develop your character. Working at home with only your pets for the company may be enjoyable at first, but will make it hard to maintain your winning mindset.

Engagement and motivation at work may be intangible and hard to measure quantitatively, but scientific research has revealed that dressing for success is not just an empty slogan. An experiment conducted at Northwestern University showed that clothes change not only other people's perception of us but also our perception of ourselves. A separate study at Hertfordshire University also did some experiments concerning the link between clothing and mindset and confirmed the findings. These experiments establish that clothes have a cognitive influence on one's behaviour. Needless to say, if you want to succeed at work, you need to dress for it.

What Should You Wear?

There are no strict dress codes when it comes to working at home: you make your own rules here. Keep in mind, however, staying consistent as much as possible. Designating an outfit for work hours does not mean that you need to prepare a suit for it, especially if wearing one makes you uncomfortable. Whatever you wear does not matter as long as it's not your usual home clothes.

CREATING A PERSONALISED DAILY ROUTINE

Habits may be powerful, but they are not easy to form and develop. Making a schedule for daily activities that you can do repetitively will help you to create good habits and abolish bad ones for a more productive life. Building a reliable daily schedule or routine is both an art and a science. The art part works with how you work personally, are you more productive earlier in the day or later? While the science part determines the things that need to get done.

Here are some useful tips when planning to make a personalised daily routine.

Make a list of daily priorities

Before anything else, write down everything you need to do daily. This is just a list of things that you usually do, not something that urgently needs doing so there is no need for organization yet. Just write down everything that you do every day, e.g. exercise, cooking food, caring for family, caring for your garden. If it's hard for you to remember everything in one sitting, bring a notebook with you and write reminders throughout the day. Always remember that, in the beginning, no task is too small.

Get specific when necessary

You can get as specific as you want if it will help you remember everything that you need to do every day. For example, you can set your alarm at six o'clock in the morning, breakfast at six-thirty, exercise at seven, and so on. It might be a very detailed schedule, but some people are more comfortable that way.

Structure your day depending on your personality and energy level

Early birds often get their tasks done before lunchtime, while night owls do theirs in the evening. In other words, you may need to think about the times when you perform your best to perform more efficiently. Doing it this way will also help you divide your tasks into the time of day that makes them more possible to complete. Mornings are concerned with activities such as getting out of the door, taking your pets out for a walk, getting the daily newspaper or magazine subscription, cooking breakfast, and taking children to school. Middays, on the other hand, are usually concerned with boring and repetitive stuff that doesn't consume too much brainpower such as answering your emails, scrubbing the bathrooms, setting appointments, and running other household chores. In the evening, you can do some planning and preparation for tomorrow, such as preparing your clothes, decluttering the rooms or workplace, and preparing tomorrow's menu.

Write it down

Documenting your routine will firstly embed it in your brain so you don't need to actively remember your diary and also give you a reference point to which you can become accountable. The much-maligned spreadsheet makes for an excellent tool for documenting your schedule. Use columns for days and rows for 30-minute slots and start filling it in from the time you want to stop working.

Test out your newly-made routine

You may test out your routine first for at least a week to make sure that everything stays in order and that you may be able to troubleshoot the underlying problems along the way. Should you encounter some issues, you can easily tweak and make adjustments to your schedule on a case-by-case basis.

STAY HEALTHY WHILE WORKING REMOTELY

Many believe that virtual workers find it easier to stay healthy compared to their office-going counterparts. After all, they can quickly whip up a healthy meal up in no time and exercise whenever they want to. However, all of these are but in theory.

In reality, many remote employees jump straight into work with their pyjamas on and tap away on their laptops. It is quite common to see them hastily pulling some fizzy soft drink and something sweet out of the fridge because they do not have enough time or energy to prepare a proper meal.

Creating a healthy work-life balance imposes a big challenge when working in an office setting all day. However, it can be equally challenging when work and life happen in the same place.

POTENTIAL BENEFITS AND HEALTH RISKS WHEN WORKING REMOTELY

Some of the various benefits of working from home are:

- Freedom
- Flexibility
- Zero commuting
- Save money
- Spending more time with loved ones
- Opportunity to do house chores

However, remote work too can have its fair share of challenges, and it will not be surprising to face the following potential health risks:

- Body pains and back issues due to bad posture
- Lack of sleep or disrupted sleeping pattern
- Obesity due to inactivity and related health issues
- Loneliness and other mental issues due to isolation

However, for every benefit, there is a potential disadvantage. For instance, you may not be distracted by colleagues visiting your desk for a juicy bit of gossip, but your children or pet would demand attention. This freedom also presents countless opportunities to procrastinate. Surfing the internet, watching Netflix, and playing with your adorable pet are just but a few things that may distract you from work.

HOW TO STAY HEALTHY WHILE WORKING REMOTELY

When working from home, it is a lot easier to forget about workouts, social interaction, sleep, and healthy eating habits. Chances of becoming careless about your health increased dramatically. However, this should not be the case. We have outlined several pointers that will help avoid the dangers and benefits of working from home.

DEVELOP YOUR DESIGNATED WORK AREA

Design of your surroundings must be conducive to a work mindset. Consider several factors such as lighting, physical comfort, ambient noise levels, and even location. All of these factors affect mental and physical health. As much as possible, your workspace should be in a quiet spot with minimal distractions.

Keep this professional space limited to professional things. Do not make it your dining room or bedroom.

Investing in a comfortable and ergonomic chair will keep you adequately aligned throughout the day. On the other hand, you may also use a standing desk to reduce the pressure on your back, giving you the option to switch between sitting and standing as your comfort levels dictate.

SCHEDULE YOUR DAY

Start the day by getting changed out of your pyjamas. Working from home makes it easier for you to forgo the morning shower and work in pyjamas all day. However, this form of neglect will be detrimental to your productivity. Taking a shower before starting to work and changing into something more presentable than sleepwear helps get you out of the casual, after-work mindset.

Aside from setting up a wakeup routine, it is also crucial to develop a structure to the day. Even a loose outline can guide you on how to stay on task and prioritise work. Although home-based work time may be shorter or longer than the traditional work time, it still must have its structure and schedule. A workable schedule must involve break times, phone calls, meetings, and realistic yet flexible windows of time to achieve the most crucial tasks in your to-do list.

When arranging your schedule, keep in mind the time of the day you feel most alert and energised as well as the time you are most unenergetic or distracted. Based on these details, organise breaks and tasks accordingly.

PREPARE MEALS AND SNACKS

Nutrition plays a vital role in a person's work performance. Proper nutrition enables us to stay focused, energised, and productive throughout the day. As it is, we find it hard to concentrate when we are hungry, or our sugar level is low.

The key to eating healthy is to store nutritious food at home. It also means that you have to limit — if not eliminate — junk foods. Cut down on refined carbs as well as sugary foods and drinks. Instead, choose whole grains, fruits, vegetables, and lean protein for your diet. The internet has vast resources to find different delicious yet nutritious recipes.

Moreover, scheduling time for breakfast, lunch, and dinner increases productivity. How? It gives a defined window to look forward to and can act as deadlines for the current task at hand, giving impetus to complete the task.

While eating, it is best to keep away from electronic devices and distractions. Practice mindful eating—taking small bites, chewing and savouring the food thoroughly, and enjoying a peaceful moment with yourself or your family.

. . .

Drink Plenty of Water

Dehydration usually leads to headaches and fatigue, which compromise concentration and productivity. Keep in mind that the brain is about 75% water (RehabChicago, 2020). It means that brain function can be adversely affected by a difference of as little as 2%. Make sure to stay hydrated by drinking water or liquids (e.g., fruit juices, herbal tea, lemon water, coconut water).

Each of us has different hydration needs. It can be based on body weight, climate, kidney function, the intensity of a workout, and many more factors. For instance, if you live in a place with a dry and humid climate, more water will need to be consumed to maintain hydration levels.

Experts recommend that a person should drink half their body weight (in ounces) daily. So, if you weigh 200 pounds, divide that by two, and you get 100. Therefore, in this example, need to drink 100 ounces (or 3 litres) of water every day.

Setting a reminder to drink water every hour dramatically helps. You can also use mobile apps, such as **Hydro Coach**, **Water Minder**, and **Daily Water Tracker Reminder,** to your advantage. As a bonus, this facilitates regular away from desk breaks.

REGULAR EXERCISE

As already mentioned, working from home gives you some allowances, including *time*. You can choose to work out even within the nine-to-five window, something your cubicle-dwelling counterparts cannot do. On the other hand, you may also find it more challenging to take working out seriously when only staying within the four corners of your home.

Making time for a sweat session provides numerous physical and mental health advantages. The activity bolsters energy levels, improves blood circulation, and boosts your overall mood. Exercising can also relieve any work-related stress. In turn, you can stay focused during your work.

The key to making a workout happen even at home is to put it in your schedule.

It is quite easy to work on your laptop without budging for hours, especially when you feel comfortable in your workspace. Nevertheless, getting up and doing some simple exercises (such as stretching, walking, jumping, and riding a stationary bike) helps you reboot your mind and body.

DEVELOP A SUPPORT SYSTEM

We know how work from home can be isolating. Without regular interaction with other people, we may tend to feel disconnected and, consequently, feel different negative emotions. To counteract the repercussions of working remotely, we need a reliable support system.

Our support system should consist of friends, family, or colleagues to communicate with online now and then. These people – especially friends and family – can encourage, inspire, and support you through thick and thin.

CREATE A LOG-OFF RITUAL

In a typical office setting, you can easily pack up your equipment and papers and head home at the end of the day. However, when you are working from home, the boundary between work and personal life can be hazy. You should not allow these two to affect each other simply because they are in the same physical space.

To draw a clear line between personal life and work, you need to design a routine that signals the end of the workday and aids the shift from professional mode to the "casual" you.

This ritual may be as simple as shutting down the computer and clearing down your desk. To make the transition even more explicit, you can leave your house and take a stroll in a park. By the time you get back, you may feel that you have just "come home from work."

MEDITATE

Meditation has helped many professionals from all over the world. In particular, mindfulness breaks help boost work performance and productivity. This type of meditation also enables you to discover yourself, including your untapped abilities.

With all the hustle and bustle, it is quite understandable that we lose our awareness within us and around us. Often, we perform things in auto-pilot, not bothering with the little things that happen in our surroundings. Eventually, this kind of attitude with life can be detrimental to our mental and physical state.

Pausing for a while to notice little things that usually do not matter can be incredibly liberating. This pause allows our minds to have a quick break and help us feel more optimistic about our situation and the world in general.

USE APPS TO STAY HEALTHY AND WELL

We now have tons of great health apps to help you to stay healthy and fit even when at home. Why not leverage them to lead a healthy lifestyle.

Practising self-care can do much to save the body and mind from the challenges imposed by working in isolation.

You may take advantage of **Calm** for meditation, **Reboot** for taking breaks, and **WaterMinder** to remind you to drink water. It is easy for remote team members to get lost in their work that even taking a few minutes to stand up from their desks to move their legs and boost metabolism are easily forgotten and neglected.

LISTEN TO MUSIC

Music can have a profound effect on the physical and emotional aspects of a person. While upbeat tunes can induce feelings that are more positive and optimistic, music with faster beats can make you more alert and aid concentration. Music with a slower tempo soothes the senses and relieves stress as it relaxes muscles and calms the mind. This is why music is very effective for stress management and relaxation.

Research findings prove that music around 60 beats per minute causes the brain to sync with the beat that creates alpha brainwaves (with frequencies from 8-14 hertz or cycles per second. The alpha brainwave state is present when one is conscious and relaxed.

For a delta brainwave of 5 hertz is required to induce sleep, one needs to relax for at least 45 minutes while listening to the soothing sound of music. Stanford University researchers had proven that listening to music seems to be able to change the functioning of the brain to the same extent as of medication (Stanford, 2006). They noted in the research that music is accessible, therefore, making it a simple tool for relieving stress.

It is a bit surprising to know that Native Americans, Celtics drums, Indian-stringed instruments, and flutes are very relaxing to the mind even when played moderately. Natural sounds like those of thunder and rain can be very relaxing when combined with light jazz, classical (e.g. the largo movement) and other soothing musical sounds.

So the kind of music that is relaxing for you depends on your choice. Also, remember that calming the mind and senses does not mean that you have to sleep. It means that your mind and body are relaxed and at rest, so when you go back to work, you can function at your best.

TAKE CARE OF YOUR MENTAL HEALTH

Since we are all using our brains when doing remote work, it is equally important to take care of them as well while we are taking care of our bodies. There are three major factors you need to focus on when taking care of your mental health – diet, sleep, and relaxation.

We are all aware that eating well can help us look and feel good. However, not all of us are aware that our mental health is greatly affected by what we eat. A well-balanced diet can help us feel more alert and think with clarity while improving our concentration and attention span.

On the other hand, an inadequate diet can result in impaired decision-making, fatigue, and slow-down reaction time. A poor diet can even lead to aggressive responses or stress and depression.

HEALTHY EATING TIPS FOR MENTAL HEALTH CARE

Steer clear of sugary snacks like fizzy drinks and sweets for they can result in inconsistencies in blood sugar levels. Also, avoid processed snack food like potato chips which can impair your ability to concentrate. Instead, eat healthy snacks when hunger strikes in-between meals, including fruits, baked sweet potatoes, and hard-boiled eggs–they can give more energy than food in a package.

When and where you eat are just as important as what you eat. Find a place to eat where you can be mindful of what you are eating. Eating in front of the television can be distracting and may cause overeating.

Eat food rich in healthy fats like coconut oil, avocado, and olive oil. They are best in supporting brain function as the brain is 60% fat.

SLEEP AND MENTAL HEALTH

It is not a secret that sleep plays a significant role in our physical and mental health. When deprived of sleep, feeling irritable and exhausted are expected but what is even more alarming are its health consequences in the long run. Lack of sleep is associated with several chronic illnesses, including type 2 diabetes, depression, and heart disease. Having good sleep hygiene and sleep practices are crucial to staying rested and getting away from daytime sleepiness.

To improve sleep and well-being, here are some actions to take.

. . .

Limit napping.

Power naps are good to recharge the mind and body, but too much of it can affect your ability to achieve quality sleep at night.

Limit nap lengths to 20-30 minutes a day, and this should not lead to sleepless nights.

Develop a Nightly Routine.

To establish a sleeping pattern, stick to a set of helpful habits like taking a bath, or have a meditation exercise to calm the senses. Having this nightly routine will help establish a good sleeping pattern which you need for healthy sleep.

Get Away from Caffeine and Stimulants Before Bedtime.

Soda, caffeine, and any other form of a stimulant can keep you wide awake. Avoid having them in the late afternoon or the evening as they can hamper the effectiveness of your sleeping routine. Having a glass of warm milk before bed has been a traditional practice through generations as a way to relieve anxiety, cultivate relaxation, and facilitate a good night's sleep.

Practice Digital Detox.

More than anything, turn off devices before bedtime. Watching TV or doing something with your phone can make it difficult to relax and go to sleep. Undergo digital detox every night to recharge your system.

Studies proved that too much technology could lead to depression, anxiety, insomnia, and impulsive behaviour ((Radiological Society of North America, Seo, & Jeong, 2017) (Pantic, 2012) (Kross et al., 2013).

RELAXATION AND MENTAL HEALTH

Relaxation helps in reducing stress and symptoms of mental health issues, including anxiety, depression, and schizophrenia. Other related benefits of relaxation include:

- Improving concentration and mood
- Lowering heart rate, breathing rate, and blood pressure
- Reducing fatigue, anger, and frustration
- Boosting confidence to deal with issues

There are various relaxation techniques to help in mental health care, which are discussed more in detail in Chapter 9. Some relaxation techniques focus on muscle control and breathing, and an example of these is progressive muscle relaxation, which involves building tension and then relaxing different muscle groups. Other techniques include visualisation, mindfulness, hypnosis, meditation and exercise.

EQUIP YOUR TEAM WITH TECH AND PRODUCTIVITY TOOLS

Communicating effectively with a remote team has always been the biggest challenge for remote team management. The nuance of a face-to-face conversation can get lost over text messaging and emails. Also, building an office culture is out of the question when you do not have a physical office in the first place.

THE ART OF COMMUNICATION

Moving to a decentralised way of working can indeed be daunting at first, but as you begin to develop an effective way of communicating with your remote team, you are sure to see the benefits.

The Global Mobile Workforce Forecast update discloses that about 40% of the world's population or over 1.87 billion workers and employees will be working mobile by 2022 (Strategy Analytics, 2016) and it can even reach up to 75% in highly developed countries like the UC according to International Data Council (IDC) ("IDC Forecasts U.S.

Mobile Worker Population to Surpass 105 Million by 2020," 2015).

With remote teams facing unique communication challenges like overcoming culture and language barriers while coordinating across time zones, building a business culture and rapport among team members won't be easy for remote managers. Added to this is the distance, which makes it harder for team members to feel like a team. If poorly managed, individual team members will feel like they're just strangers working on the same project from different places.

Here are some of the ways to bridge the virtual gap between remote team members so they can work efficiently even while physically apart from each other.

Have Regular Live Meetings

Trust is vital to establish rapport between team members. If you are interacting through phone or via messages, you can't see their expressions, gestures, and other nonverbal cues. Therefore, you have to make it a point to complement conventional email and messaging system with regular video conferences to allow team members to view each other.

It will be hard for team members to be productive without established working relationships, and relationships are hard to build without these live meetings at the start. Live meetings help nurture and grow the relationship between you and each of the team members over time.

Create Opportunities for Connection

Remote teams have no natural opportunities to bond

after office hours or lunch breaks so remote managers need to actively create ways to inspire and motivate each other to connect. Rachel Valdez, head of PowertoFly – Global Talent Management said that the secret formula to building a killer remote team is disruptive kindness. In the company, they organise the TGIIF (Thank God It's Inspirational Friday) meetings where everyone is encouraged to share stories of what had inspired them and what they are looking forward to during the weekend.

For remote team members, points like these make all the difference, and it's not surprising to see an increase in productivity and general well-being for remote teams who have this kind of remote activity.

Drive Collaboration via Messaging Technologies

When Zogby Analytics conducted a study, they found out that about 41% of remote teams are still coordinating using text messaging, Facebook messenger, and Skype instead of using a given mobile platform specifically designed for remote communication and management. Doing so resulted in information loss when teams, individuals, and management use different communication channels. Backchannels also put the company at risk because communication and collaboration are happening on free platforms were security is sometimes compromised. Stacy Eppstein, the CEO of Zinc, felt that while 71 per cent of managers keep up to date on work news, only 40 per cent of the staff feels the same (Peek, 2018).

Set Up Communication Guidelines

Another key to working remotely is setting up clear guidelines on communication. This guideline need not be difficult or complex.

Just explain the sort of communication is appropriate and when it is of use. An example is when using Slack for general chatting, but all final decisions and official matters need to be recorded through email or on an appropriate ticket. You may also ask your team members to send official documents during office hours, and for emergency or urgent communication, it must be via phone calls.

Also, set guidelines of appropriate communication relating to explicit language, profanity, and subject topics.

Beat Buhlman, former General Manager of Evernote said that it's always important to set rules when it comes to the use of communication tools. You must be specific of how and when to use them like why do we have to write emails? When do we chat and when do we receive calls? Although having an open line of communication is beneficial, it also has its definite drawbacks. It can be counterproductive to send project notifications via chats as team members are likely to get distracted by constant notifications. They are also likely to lose important information in a long thread.

Emails are perfect for sending information, but when use in collaboration, especially when the topic requires clarity and sensitivity, or when parties can benefit from a vibrant exchange of ideas, better schedule a call instead.

Teach Team Members to Contextualise Communication

When communicating with the rest of the team digitally, you will never know what is happening at the end of the line while you are transmitting the message or talking with them verbally. The person on the other end of the line may simply respond with "yes". It is not because they are not interested in what you are saying, but it could be that they are in a situation where prevents them from further elaborating their response. Without really understanding the reason behind this, this may create a misunderstanding. That's why remote teams have to avoid assumptions as psychological safety is more important.

Even when you are in the habit of merely responding "yes" or "no" to a simple question, you must not fail to remember that the person at the other end needs to understand the situation you're in so they can properly analyze your responses.

Since building rapport is essential in any aspect of a business, and you can only build it through proper communication, it is crucial to prevent any form of misunderstanding between remote team members. Saying so when you're distracted, offended, or confused is essential to avoid it. Resentment grows eventually if underlying issues are not addressed immediately.

Communication is never that easy, even in a traditional workplace. However, this difficulty is even more magnified when workers are in different locations and time zones, and with different personalities and cultures.

You can't communicate with your team in a nonverbal way because you can't be together in person, but still, communication is what binds one to the rest of the group, and with an active communication network, the purpose and goal are shared by everyone who is working towards their achievement and with deep commitment.

TOOLS AND STRATEGIES FOR REMOTE WORK

A research study on productivity revealed that remote workers are more productive and more satisfied with their jobs compared to their contemporaries ("To Raise Productivity, Let More Employees Work from Home," 2014). Businesses are also able to save much on overhead costs for space, office supplies, and other equipment when employing a remote team of workers who have their facilities to complete projects. So now, many companies all over the world realise that remote work can help in productivity, and business can continue as usual regardless of workers' locations.

However, some difficulties and challenges will emerge alongside remote work. So, when contemplating long-term remote work as an option for your business, you need to consider investing in the right tools and equipment to oversee work, manage projects, and communicate effectively for productivity.

You can never find the best method to work remotely. The tools and techniques you can utilise to manage your daily projects and tasks will be determined by your style of work and the policies implemented by your company.

If you think that there is such a thing as an exclusive set of remote worker tools, you are entirely wrong. To be honest, the tools that long-distance employees use do not differ from those commonly used in the office. Moreover, the tools deemed effective by someone else might not be practical for you. However, it would help you identify where to begin and discover what is absent from your remote work process.

Let me guide you to find the right innovative solutions

for your remote work. In this section, we are sharing proven methods and tools that can enhance your work process.

Internet Speed

Internet speed can have a massive impact on the productivity levels of remote workers. A report by the Washington Post explained that locations with faster internet speed produce a higher GDP per capita while those with slow internet speed indicates lower GDP per capita. (The Washington Post & Fung, 2014).

Remote workers need high-speed internet to be connected and productive. Allow your remote team to use internet speed tools to make sure that their internet speed is high enough to share large files, host video conferences, and use online tools. These tools are available for free, easy to use, and helps you gauge your team's internet needs.

Good internet speed for an average worker is about 30 Mbps. Some have less while others will require more. But 30 Mbps is a good point to start.

The use of internet speed could vary for everyone based on what you do online and on how many devices are connected to your network. With a good internet speed, you can do whatever you want online without limitations.

To put it simply, here is a breakdown of typical internet speed ranges and what you can do with them.

0-5 Mbps

- Searching online
- Checking emails
- Streaming music one just one device

5-40 Mbps

- Video calling with Skype or Face Time
- Streaming video with just one device
- Online gaming for one player

40-100 Mbps

- Multiplayer online gaming
- Streaming HD video on a few devices
- Downloading large files

100-500 Mbps

- Gaming online for multiple players
- Downloading files quickly
- Streaming video in UHD on numerous screens

500-1000 plus Mbps

- Doing a lot of almost anything

COMMUNICATION AND COLLABORATION METHODS

Email has been one of the more significant communication methods, especially in a work setting. However, it can be quite a hassle when you need to convey everything using this method.

To keep in touch with your team in real-time, you can use cloud-based collaboration tools or message boards such as the following:

Workplace (by Facebook)

Facebook added a suite of tools that benefits professionals like you. You can create groups and host live chats to collaborate with your entire team. It is also beneficial if you are working with people from other companies. You can seamlessly chat, connect, and collaborate without the nuisances of email. Facebook offers it for free to $3 per month for each user.

Microsoft Teams

Teams, as a part of the premium Office 365 subscriptions, is a full communication and service collaboration suite for Windows users. You can make VOIP (Voice over Internet Protocol) and video calls within Teams, share work from other 365 apps, as well as direct and group message other Windows users.

. . .

Google Hangouts

Hangouts may be focused on video messaging but also has the capability for instant messaging. This app works primarily when your team heavily uses Google Docs and Google Drive since it is easy to integrate Hangouts in these said apps. A G-Suite subscription starts at $5 per month.

Flock

Flock is known as a workplace chat app that features audio and video calls, instant chat, as well as built-in notes, polls, reminders, and code snippets. It offers free and paid plans, with the former allowing 10,000 searchable messages while the latter unlocks practical features such as unlimited message history and screen sharing.

Slack

An award-winning collaboration and messaging app, **Slack**, serves remote teams as an alternative to email in the workplace. It offers *Free plan*, *Standard plan*, *Plus plan*, and *Enterprise Grid plan* (which caters to extra-large businesses or for those in regulated industries). Slack brings the team to a single place to communicate and share files. It also highlights various tools that help everyone work faster and more effectively.

With remote work, you can't just pop over to someone's desk to ask a question or share a document, and with Slack, you can send direct chats to a specific team member and even create focused channels for different teams to collaborate over time. However, when you need to focus on something, you can set notifications to snooze or also connect a calendar app to automatically shift status when in a meeting or when at work. Slack is quick, simple, easy to use, and can be customised to fit the exact need of your team.

Slack works perfectly for anyone managing a team of long-distance employees.

On the other hand, software developers may need to utilise these tools for *pair programming*:

Fleep

A fantastic app for people who work across organisational units, **Fleep** offers a free plan and business plan, which starts at €5 per month for each user. You can also utilise its messaging feature to communicate with people outside Fleep.

Chanty

Great for small and medium-sized teams, Chanty is a simple and straightforward chat tool that does not restrict its searchable message history. Chanty also allows you to communicate in both private and public channels as well as through one-to-one conversations. It organises tasks, files, links, and discussions into different folders via its *Teambook* feature. It offers a free plan for a team with a maximum of ten members, while its paid plans start at $3 per month for each user.

You don't have to depend on a single video conference tool. Sometimes, there are connectivity issues that can affect the quality of your communication. To be on the safe side, try different communication tools.

In particular, the *screen sharing* feature is considered a

must-have for any remote team. Under a typical workplace, teammates usually approach each other to look over something. Screen sharing allows you to do just that, albeit virtually. The feature lets you share what you are currently seeing with other people in your team. You can use it to brainstorm, outline your ideas, and set up wireframes.

Meanwhile, if you don't want to call a meeting to pinpoint a particular button on a website, you can use a tool like **Evernote**. With it, you can take screenshots and edit the image by adding arrows, shapes, highlights, or texts to show your points of interest.

Providing the facility for remote collaboration on files and documents should also be taken into serious consideration. Creating articles, presentations, and spreadsheets in a cloud-based tool permits your teammates to review and contribute them in real-time. You do not need to upload and download files via emails, with tens of versions of the same document repeatedly.

Google's ingenious solution by introducing **Google Drive** has allowed us to create and edit online documents in real-time. As such, team members can directly write, edit, proofread and feedback the documents or files without waiting on each other most of the time. If Google isn't your cup of tea, you can try others such as **OnlyOffice, S Suite Office Software, Documents To Go**, and **Microsoft OneDrive**.

If your area is about design, visual content, and prototyping, know that you also have collaboration tools such as:

Figma

A great tool where teams design together, Figma is a cloud-based design tool emphasizing team collaboration.

InVision

A popular tool, InVision, provides the best possible digital product experience. It has intuitive tools for design, ideation, design management, and prototyping. Clients can also provide feedback in the form of comments, and even check the project in real-time.

Canva

Canva has made designing and lay-outing easy with its unique drag-and-drop feature. It allows individuals and teams to design and create everything—from logos, business cards and presentations.

Webflow

Webflow is especially useful to web developers and designers. It helps you build your animations and interactions using the same tool you use in your web design work. Your team and clients can directly give you feedback all in the same place.

Marvel

Marvel is a collaborative design platform used to design, create wireframes, prototyping, user-testing, and inspecting designs in a single place.

. . .

Codeshare

Like its name, Codeshare allows developers to "share" codes in real-time with just a browser. It features a code editor for troubleshooting, writing, collaboration and teaching. Using the platform, you can easily pair and troubleshoot programs with your colleagues.

AWS Cloud9

A cloud-based IDE (integrated development environment), AWS Cloud9 enables users to run, write, and debug codes using a browser. It features debuggers, code editor, and terminal. You can work on your projects anywhere with just a device connected to the internet. Likewise, your team will experience a seamless workflow using this app. You can monitor each other's inputs and pair program in real-time.

Teletype for Atom

Teletype for Atom establishes the concept of real-time portals for sharing workspaces. You can make collaboration and edits all in real-time.

Floobits

Floobits flaunts its ability to do more than just screen sharing. You can share terminals, video chat, screen share, and edit all at the same time. It currently supports Emacs, Sublime Text, Neovim, IntelliJ IDEA, and Atom.

Visual Studio Live Share

The software enables you to share projects with your peers or colleagues from the comfort of your Visual Studio Code. It does not matter what type of app you're creating, which OS you use, or which language you program. You do not have to clone a repo or generate an environment just to get sharing.

ORGANISING TASKS

Long-distance project management requires effective tools to make development workflows seamless. Since interactions with your team happen daily, you need to know which tools can bring the results needed by the end of the day.

There are various project management apps available in the digital marketplace. All you should do is to determine which works best for your team. Here are some of the best project management software:

Asana

Asana is a great tool that will help your team updated with your workflow. It enables you to generate to-do lists, monitor tasks via the *project board*, make deadline reminders, comment on your team members' posts, and send requests to the entire team. Employers also utilise it to keep track of your projects' progress. I find Asana is better suited to smaller sized projects.

Paymo

Paymo is a full-featured online project management software that offers convenience. It helps freelancers and teams to create team schedules, monitor work time, manage various tasks, and bill clients in a single space.

Trello

This project management tool allows its users to share tasks, projects, ideas, and many more in a single interface in real-time. You can categorise and order texts, drawings, photos, and prototypes through a system of post-it notes. Furthermore, you can easily monitor the pipeline of your project and set appointment reminders. Trello is better suited to simpler or higher-level tracking of projects.

Wrike

Wrike permits users full visibility and control of all your team's tasks and projects. It is widely popular for those who love the minimalist user interface. The app keeps tabs on dependencies, dates, and time connected with projects and also manages resources and assignments.

Jira

Jira by Atlassian is part of a fully-fledged suite of online applications that provides extreme flexibility in how you track and manage agile projects. Jira is possibly the best option for large scale projects.

FILE OR ASSET SHARING

Sharing or storing documents and images securely on a platform that you trust can be difficult, especially when it is difficult to revisit and organise documents outside of specific assignments or projects. For this, you need to choose a file-sharing platform that will make this process easier for you and your team.

Google Drive

Studies disclosed that it takes about eight searches before one can find the correct documents and information you need to complete a given task. This task can even be more frustrating for remote workers, which is why sending multiple versions of a file to several remote team members is a disaster that is bound to happen sooner or later (Bernstein, 2013).

For easier collaboration in real-time and creating documents, Google Drive can be useful as you and your team members can work on a file at the same time. So someone in the team stores files in the Drive, it can be accessible to everyone. Google Drive is free to use for those with a Gmail account, and there's no limit to the number of collaborators.

STORING FILES IN A SAFE PLACE

Any project you are working on must have a safe and protected place to store files. Dealing with remote work entails a straightforward system for file management. Moreover, backing these files up with a strong password is paramount.

The project management platform you use must have a division for *Files* and *Attachments* where you can find all the files and documents that are associated with your digital workplace. You have to develop a sorting system which makes it easier for you to locate—let's say—a document you worked on six months ago.

In case that your app or software does not have a feature that stores files for a long time or unlimited storage, then you can pair it with tools such as Dropbox, OneDrive, Google Drive, and Box.

Another thing you must never take lightly is CYBERSECURITY.

Even if your devices are usually used for work, you use them during your free time, too. Whatever you watch, click, or download, particularly when connected to a public Wi-Fi, can potentially harm or corrupt your work files.

According to an iPass security report, more than 60% of all security incidents associated with Wi-Fi happened in coffee shops. Furthermore, the CIOs (Chief Information Officers) believe that remote employees are frequently the cause of mobile security issues.

You may not intend to wipe out your entire files simply because you unwittingly clicked on a link from a spam email, but it can happen. For this, you may want to apply safety measures like the following:

- Never leave your laptop unattended, especially when you're working from a public space.
- If possible, do not use a public Wi-Fi connection since they are not secured. Tethering to your own mobile phone is much more within your control.
- Do not use identical passwords on all your accounts (e.g., Your Facebook, Canva, Google, and bank apps share the same password).
- Secure all of your devices with strong passwords

that contain lower and uppercase letters, numbers, and special characters.
- Change your password every time security issues arise (e.g., when Facebook notifies you that someone is trying to access your account).
- Use password managers for additional security and strong password suggestions.
- Activate two-factor authentication whenever there is an available option for it.
- Install credible antivirus software and update it regularly.
- Never download software or apps from untrustworthy websites or those without an authenticity license.
- Update your installed software regularly since most updates often have a security reason behind them.
- Use a reliable VPN service to keep your internet traffic encrypted.
- Never access your work accounts from other people's devices or any public computer.

TRACKING WORK

As a remote worker or someone who monitors other remote workers, you should know how to follow work and its development stages.

Time tracking is a system of keeping track and recording the time you spend on a project, task, or activity. This method can be accomplished using a digital stopwatch or an automatic time tracker.

There is a marginal difference when it comes to work

procedure, whether you are monitoring time automatically or manually. You should remember these options when you want to switch from one in favour of the other. If you aren't still using one or are looking for the right tracking tools that suit you best, here are some of the most popular ones:

- Paymo
- Time Doctor
- Toggl
- Harvest
- Timely
- TimeCamp
- RescueTime
- Workpuls

These automatic time monitoring tools can record every activity you perform on your computer. It keeps track of any apps, files, browser tabs, and even idle time. Simply turn the timer on at the beginning of the day, then stop it when you are done for the day.

Let's say you often work with multiple projects at the same time. The trackers can match your activities to the right project and task by the end of the day. It also works great if you need to recognise your significant distractions.

Aside from the tools mentioned above, you can also utilise the time trackers on your smartphone. You may have to start and stop your time each time, but it gives you better control of your time. You can send your recorded hours into a timesheet. Timesheets are your virtual or physical proof of your work time.

Remote workers and managers need to consider integrating time reports to their ensemble of virtual tools. Time reports are visual work summaries that present how you spend time, resources, and money. Having these in a remote team is an essential tool for cutting down on administrative discussions, activities, and tasks. Remote managers or team leaders will easily monitor if team members have time for another job or are overloaded with work.

Since team members often rely on each other, time constraints are crucial. Project managers cannot start planning without precisely learning what needs doing.

MANAGING TIME

Time management is tied directly into productivity, and while the traditional work environment helps workers and employees make the distinction of the time to focus, staying and working at home can remove this. Here are some apps that might help you maintain focus.

Timely

Some case studies have shown that using a tracking system to keep tabs on how workers are spending their time is not only beneficial to managers who want to have an idea of how their workers are spending their working hours but also to significantly increase their productivity ("Billable Hours for Professional Services - Replicon Case Study," n.d.).

With **Timely** – a time-tracking device, it will be easier for you to keep track of your remote workers' hours and monitor how long it takes them to finish an assigned task. With the app running in the background of their computers, you can maintain a digital log of all projects. You set goals, compare recorded time against estimates, and organising tasks based on priorities. With Timely's Professional Plan, you can manage your team members on the same account.

Miro

According to a report by Fisher Vista, employees who are highly engaged in the company they work for are 87% more likely to remain with their employer that those workers who are disengaged. To make your team members feel that they are a part of the company is a significant step in preventing a high turnover rate among your remote team (Replicon, 2000).

Remote work may be less stressful than commuting every day from one's home to the workplace, but you are sure to miss out on the whiteboard brainstorming sessions. **Miro** – a visual collaboration app can provide your team with the digital version of these team-bonding opportunities. They can brainstorm, create diagrams, brainstorm, conduct research, add sticky notes, among many other things, plus the app is free up to three members.

Work-Life Balance

Work-Life balance is essential to all remote workers, including you and your family. Providing your employees with tools that help them establish a healthy balance can improve your productivity level as it ensured each team member to have enough rest, exercise, social interaction, and unwind after work to relax and recoup. It shows that you care for them and their well-being which could drive them to participate actively and be satisfied in their work to make them stay with you for years to come.

Here are some options to help them live healthy lives after work.

Nike Training Club

This app has specific workouts designed for a certain amount of time you're interested in working out. It also allows you to select which muscle group you'd like to target. You also have the option to work with your body weight, free weights, or any other workout equipment available in your home.

Daily Burn

Here's another app that offers personalised workout plans consisting of many activities, including yoga, kickboxing, barre and dumbbell strength training. All you have to do to start is to answer a personalised quiz about your typical workout routine and current physical status.

There are too many apps available for free. Just choose the one that can work right for you. Staying active while working remotely will help you stay physically healthy and clear your mind of fog and cobwebs. With a team of energetic and clear-headed remote workers under your management, expect your productivity levels to be higher than ever.

BULLET JOURNALING

It is usual nowadays to rely on technology whenever we want to become more productive, hence the rise of self-improvement and productivity apps. Many people use multiple apps across their devices, whether be it wearable gadgets, smartphones, tablets, or computers.

This surge in high-tech productivity, however, is also fueling a low-tech revival, one of which is none other than bullet journaling.

What is Bullet Journaling?

In a literal sense, a bullet journal is an entire organisational system in a single notebook. Aside from a notepad, it also includes a calendar, a to-do list, and a diary. You can use the bullet journal as you see fit since most of its pages are blank, compared to regular journals with pre-printed pages. The reason why bullet journals are popular is that they can adapt to the way you work. You can even fill it with fancy lettering or stay pure.

Bullet Journal Structure

Bullet journaling has a recommended basic layout for beginners for organisational purposes. At the beginning of each bullet journal, you can write an index for easy reference. Next, you can create a daily, weekly, monthly, and a future log for your tasks before writing notes and creating a calendar. You can also log and track the tasks that you have and haven't done daily. And finally, you can review everything you wrote on a weekly or monthly basis, and in case that you forgot to do something, you can either cancel or just include it to the next month's goals.

Bullet Journaling Pros and Cons

Those who use bullet journals are said to be able to achieve their goals, declutter their mind, and eliminate unnecessary tasks, all at the same time. This aspect of mindfulness is another reason for the bullet journal's popularity, as well as being an easy way to focus on what is important. It also gives its users a holistic view of their work and lives.

The primary downside about bullet journaling, however, is that they tend to be time-consuming. Since most of its contents are blank, you need to set up everything yourself, starting from numbering the pages up to regularly updating your index. The time spent here could have been used to do your tasks so it could be somewhat frustrating. In addition to that, bullet journals will introduce you to new concepts such as modules, logs, collections, and migrations, which can be quite intimidating for those who have limited knowledge, especially newbies. Needless to say, you will have to invest some time to adapt and get used to this organisation methodology.

Bullet Journaling Alternatives

While bullet journaling's popularity is undeniable, it is worth considering every available option before putting your energy into it. Bullet journaling is only effective if one knows how to use it properly. If your only goal is to become as productive as possible, there are many alternative apps out there that you can use instead. Listed below are some of those.

Work Diaries

You might want to consider keeping a work diary or

productivity journal if you prefer writing things down. It may be somewhat analogue compared to a bullet journal, but they are considerably less intense. In addition to that, writing things down is good for mental health and, just like with bullet journal, it helps people clarify their goals as well as focus their minds. Work diaries tend to be the most overlooked of all the time management tools available for use by people. If done very well, a work diary becomes an invaluable resource for managing one's productivity and professional development in detail, highlighting new opportunities, successes, and setbacks.

Artificial Intelligence-Based Assessments and Insights

There are apps nowadays that utilise artificial intelligence to break down and assess your performance for you. Apps like **Dewo** can multitask, assess your focus quality, and determine how much deep work you can do each day. These programs can even help you maintain your productivity by blocking distracting notifications as well as schedule meetings around your available focused time.

Automatic Time Trackers

These apps create a productivity log of your daily tasks, starting from the time you spent making your bed up to the time you spent while sleeping. Using time trackers also lets you review your past performances, making you approach situations using various methods. Unlike journals, they are entirely objective, meaning that they reveal the intricacies of your work rather than how you think you should work. This

HOW TO KEEP A WORK DIARY CORRECTLY

There are three various ways of keeping a work diary, which vary depending on its detail and effort requirement. For those who write lengthy details about their performance, there are long-form analogy types. On the other hand, to those who want to keep track of their progress with a little effort as much as possible, automatic digital types are available for use.

Listed below are the three types of work diary, which are classified according to their use:

Activity Log

This is a record of everything you worked on in very minute details, starting from the time of planning up to its completion. This type shows the number of things that you achieved, which is quite useful when observing progress daily. Being one of the best product management tools, an activity log lays out inefficiencies and distractions so you can observe and troubleshoot them later, as well as improve your work focus. A human may not be capable of keeping a record of every detail in his work, so an automatic tracking tool was invented for such a situation.

Work Journal

Using a work journal may be somewhat traditional, but it is still a very effective way of keeping oneself in check. This is where you literally 'write your heart out', documenting everything in as much detail as possible. It is the best method of processing events, noting feedbacks, and materialising development goals. What's more, is that a work journal allows you to vent out your anger and frustrations towards work in private, which can be later refined into various actions such as personality improvements, training opportunities, and much more. Keep in mind to take note of every detail and celebrate your victories whenever you can.

The List

A short-hand analogy approach compared to the previous two, a list type work diary is just a breakdown of whatever you achieved on a daily or weekly basis. It is merely a collection of main events during your work that needs careful observation. By using this method, you can just list whatever thing you want to achieve in a day or a week, then comparing the notes of what you accomplished after that time. This list is most useful if you want a relatively high-level overview of your work performance or if you just want to focus on working on your priorities.

BOOST YOUR TEAMS MORALE

Keeping a positive and competitive atmosphere in any workplace—physical or virtual— should be any manager's top priority. However, bolstering the morale of a remote team can be a little more challenging than the traditional setup. The reason—the strategies which are deemed to be effective in a conventional office setting might not be as effective for employees working remotely.

In a traditional workplace, after-work drinks, team lunches, and office banter can quickly bolster employee morale. However, virtual workers miss out on these things. As a manager, how do you fill in the gap to ensure a healthy work environment for your team?

Let us help you with these morale-boosting strategies. These essential points will surely help keep the vibe in your team going:

DESIGN YOUR RECOGNITION AND APPRECIATION STRATEGY

Workers always want to feel appreciated; hence, having a strong employee recognition strategy is a must for any manager or leader. Appreciation and recognition present a nice boost of morale and can gain a drastic effect on your team's performance. So, how do you show the gratitude and recognition your team needs despite the physical gap?

A study comprising 13,000 American workers showed that 50% of these participants value words of affirmation the most; 25% of these participants enjoyed quality time with their colleagues; 20% favoured kindness; the remaining 5% would rather receive physical gifts.

From this same group, about 35% of remote team members confessed that they prefer time with colleagues compared to 25% of the in-house staff. Since remote employees often feel disconnected from the rest, mere words may not hold the same intensity. Surmise to say, remote managers, are encouraged to be more creative in forming their recognition strategies for their remote staff.

You do not have to dish out a pricey gift every single time to show your appreciation. A simple thank you note, or a direct, but public, thank you during one of your virtual meetings will also do the trick. Being a manager does not limit you from being only that. You can be a friend or confidante also. Kindness is something every soul needs, and when freely given, you will generally get kindness in return. Now, all of these may sound too simple, but these are proven methods that bring out real results.

All you need to do is to keep your eyes open for every opportunity and be ready to give the appreciation and recognition they deserve. Appreciating your team increases their self-worth, confidence, and positivity. According to a Gallup poll, almost 70% of employees are willing to work harder when recognised and appreciated (Gallup, Inc., 2020).

Let us share with you some ideas on how you can show your appreciation even though you are miles away from your remote staff:

SEND THEM LOVE WITH SOME SWAG

You may be the most dedicated manager on the planet. If you are in a typical workplace with your staff, they can easily see and feel it. Unfortunately, distance is one of your most significant obstructions. What you need is to be a little bit more creative than usual.

If you have worked hard enough to generate a rich culture with your team, then you need to show it off. Send your team members some love with SWAG (Stuff We All Get) — mugs, laptop stickers, t-shirts or customised pens — to thank your team for their efforts. After all, everybody loves free stuff. Plus, they will feel the love and care you are transmitting through the gifts.

BE SPECIFIC WITH YOUR PRAISE AND RECOGNITION

Employee recognition generates employee engagement. Hence, it is critical for managers to provide feedback to their team. While this may mean creating more personalised messages, this small effort will delight an employee.

Remember that employees love to hear that they are valued and that their efforts are recognised. When these individuals meet or exceed expectations, you, as their manager, must send them a message that explicitly mentions their achievement.

OFFER EXTRA TRAINING AND PROFESSIONAL DEVELOPMENT

Even though some employees are content with performing the same tasks daily, know that others may be aspiring to get into another level. These individuals are not afraid of getting more responsibility, knowledge, and opportunities. For this reason, offering extra training, online educational seminars, or providing them access to sites that can help them grow their experience will be a great help.

If you have already designed your remote training program, then you are ahead of the curve. You can take this into a brand new level by improving the professional development of your remote team. It may mean:

- Providing them one-on-one sessions with educators and mentors
- Sending them to various trade conferences and seminars
- Encouraging them to enrol for online courses
- Guide and advise them about career development

Now, most of these seem costly, but it is a good investment for your company and business that can reap many benefits. In some cases, this employee-friendly program is tax-deductible.

Helping your employees obtain knowledge to expose them to career advancement opportunities is considered a form of appreciation and recognition. You are pushing them to exceed their limits simply because you acknowledge that they can do it.

SEND THEM PERSONALISED THANK YOU NOTES

Group emails are a convenient way to communicate ideas, tasks, and expectations to your team. However, this method cannot be considered as a thoughtful way to show appreciation. Send your team members an individualised message highlighting their accomplishments and contributions to the team for the past sprint, quarter or year.

Many supervisors and managers believe that this simple tactic helps bolster the morale of employees. It shows that you, their manager, appreciate each of your members as an individual, and they are not just someone working in front of a computer.

Send Snail Mail

A personalised letter set in letterhead stationery can be a breath of fresh air in today's high-tech world. Your remote staff might be surprised to receive some snail mail that is not a bill, much more when the content is all about appreciation. The letter also shows that you have gone the extra mile to convey your gratitude for their work and truly appreciate their presence in your team.

Present Your Staff Online

Most remote companies have a dedicated page about their company, including the people working with them. Showcasing them gives your audience a friendlier and more trustworthy "feel" about your team. In the same effect, you can create a small personal blurb plus a photo of each of your remote workers. Showing that you are proud that they are part of your team, plus this helps them feel like they part of something larger and more significant.

Recognise Their Accomplishments

Life milestones or achievements are always meant to be shared with the people who matter in our lives. Although you may not have physically met your remote staff yet, valuing their life achievements shows you care about them. Mentioning your workers' accomplishments on message boards or virtual meetings is another incredible way to show how much you appreciate them. If they get married, have a baby, or finished an online course, be ready to recognise these events.

IMPROVE COLLABORATION

Collaboration greatly amplifies workplace performance. Teams that work together remain engaged in their tasks 64% longer than those who work by themselves ("Cues of working together fuel intrinsic motivation," 2014). Moreover, closely-knit teams tend to show higher engagement levels, lower fatigue levels, and higher success rates.

Although physical distance may be a problem, there are digital tools that make collaborative working much more accessible. What your team members need is a mere perception or cue that they are working together. It shouldn't be an arduous task for any remote manager to facilitate social coordination and cooperation.

Aside from providing a platform for your team to connect and communicate, you should also dedicate time to be with them—at least virtually. Beyond professional relationship, you can be a friend they can depend on during troubled times, even outside of work. Do your best to be systematic in providing instructions and resolving complex issues as soon as your team brings them up.

BE CONSIDERATE OF TIME

Another way to enhance the morale of your virtual team members is to be considerate of their schedules, particularly if they are working in different time zones. As much as possible, try to hold meetings at hours that won't necessitate them to stay up late or get up extra early.

Remote work requires a certain degree of flexibility that allows you to create schedules as you deem appropriate, but many remote workers never make most of this opportunity. Encourage your team to take frequent break times and build them into a structured schedule.

Most remote workers tend to work for as long as possible, especially when they are already "in the zone." It might sound impressive, but working without intervals can be exhausting. As it is, exhaustion is disastrous for one's mental health and productivity.

Remember the proverb, "All work and no play makes Jack a dull boy?" This adage is especially true to remote workers who are more susceptible to work under the pressure of delivering work on time, all the time. As a manager, you should understand that despite your team working from home, this kind of set up does not exempt them from other obligations.

Persuade your team to take regular breaks. This act alone lets them realise that their manager considers their well-being, thereby boosting their work morale.

ENSURE EQUAL OPPORTUNITY FOR ALL

Being a manager entails you to validate that the virtual employees under you would gain the same opportunities as their traditional office contemporaries enjoy. This goes beyond simple recognition and appreciation. It is about career opportunities and expansion. Fair salary, excellent benefits, and flexible work options can also keep remote workers in high spirits.

GENUINELY CARE FOR YOUR TEAM

A remote manager must show that they sincerely care on both professional and personal levels. Showing that you care isn't all about monetary or material rewards. Throwing a simple virtual birthday party can increase the morale of your team members. They will feel more valued and cared regardless of the distance between them.

In a study, workers who believe that they are heard usually perform 4.6 times much better than their regular performance (Schwartz, n.d.). By consistently getting your team's insights, ideas, and opinions, you help them feel important. More importantly, do not forget to thank them for sharing their suggestions. When you deal with their issues, it makes them feel that they have been heard. As a result, they are more likely to remain motivated.

DO TEAM BUILDING ACTIVITIES TOGETHER

When workers often see each other in an office-based setting, it is easy for them to form connections on a personal level. However, establishing bonds in this level can be challenging when the team members are working from different time zones or buildings.

To counterbalance, a manager should incorporate team building activities into the team's routine. Team building allows virtual teams to establish a connection and mutual respect, which are two of the most crucial aspects of a team's success. Adding a bit of comic relief daily helps fight tedium and isolation, which are often associated with working from home.

Virtual team building covers several activities, programs, and games that are designed to enhance human interaction in a digital work environment. These may include icebreaker questions to incite excitement and fun to remote work. Let us give you some icebreaker samples:

- Quick questions and fill in the blanks such as, "If I won the lottery, I would..." or "What would you do if (a celebrity) asked you for a date?" or "Take a coin out of your pocket and tell us something that happened in the year that is on the coin."
- Take a picture of something and add it to your virtual board to share.
- Ask your members to share two truths and a lie about them. Each member can vote which of the three statements is the LIE. Once everybody has voted, reveal the right answers and give your

members the time for follow-up questions for interaction.
- Make trivia games, vocabulary enhancement, or puzzles. You can try **Kahoot** for more virtual games.

Feel free to provide rewards or prizes to make the games or activities more enticing. This method enables your team to be more competitive and emotionally closer at the same time.

DON'T BE TOO STRICT, ENCOURAGE VIRTUAL COFFEE BREAKS

Coffee breaks within the office develop social interactions. It is something which work-from-home employees miss out due to the nature of their work. The lack of quality face-to-face time debilitates the interpersonal aspects of social interaction between team members. In turn, it can be quite detrimental to teamwork, making some employees feel detached and unmotivated.

You, as a manager, should create strategies to compensate one-on-one team meetings to prevent isolation and burnout. One of the best ways is promoting virtual coffee breaks, which are video calls that team share during breaks to socialise. This strategy helps your team members to learn about each other, build better relationships, and keep the camaraderie solid. Tell your team to dedicate a few minutes —even hours—to have these calls while they grab their favourite snack or drink. Only one rule should be set for these particular calls: no shop talk!

RESPECT THE CULTURE AND BACKGROUNDS OF YOUR TEAM MEMBERS

Integrating appreciation and rewards into your remote efforts entails detailed attention to your remote staff's cultural background. This detail is especially important when your team hails from various parts of the globe. Keep a comprehensive calendar—calendar apps do wonders—to help you list each member's cultural, national and religious holidays. Always keep your members' background in mind when you plan to reward them.

As you start to customise your reward system for your remote workforce, remember to stay consistent. When you construct and implement this system, you also begin to market it as a company standard. You will gradually become a modern organisation that values connection and camaraderie, yet promotes worker autonomy and independence at the same time.

RESPECT PRIVATE TIME

Just because your team members are working remotely and have a flexible schedule, it does not mean that you can call on them anytime. You can't just intrude on their privacy any moment you want. It is therefore crucial that you discuss this with them as part of your communication schedule. Chart out a plan that will work with both of you and make sure that you all adhere to it. This means resisting the temptation to call any of your remote team members when you know that it is outside of their working hours. Another thing, since your team members may come from different locations, it is also vital that you check your time difference. Use an app that will help you determine their local time before calling. You may also choose to leave a text message via chat or email so it can reach them and they can quickly read it as soon as they're back to work.

When what you want to convey to them is urgent or what we can consider an emergency where communication can't wait for the next office hour, it can be treated as an exception to the general rule and procedures.

Respecting your team privacy will motivate them to give their best performance at work because they know you care and respect them.

SHOW THEM YOU AREN'T AN EXCEPTION TO THE RULE

Leaders who are well-loved and respected by their teammates are usually those they find easily relatable.

It means, in some ways, you must show them that you aren't above the rule. When you have set guidelines that must be followed, team members are expecting you to follow them just as you expect them to follow it. Being in a team, whether remote or not, means that you are all present to work on a common goal and should, therefore, cooperate in all things that will lead to the achievement of the defined target.

Sometimes, leaders fail because they tend to show their teammates that they are above them in all aspects. This kind of leadership tends to keep your teammates apart from you and discourage them from doing their best which eventually affect the team's productivity.

RECOGNISE AND POSITIVELY DEAL WITH POTENTIAL MENTAL ISSUES

You may have on your remote team some workers who are experiencing some mental health issues like stress, anxiety or depression due to the nature of their work. Although, depending on the severity of their symptoms, many can still work with little impact on productivity. Generally, it's the supportive performance of the management that helps much with their continued productivity.

By applying sensitivity, positivity, and constructive solutions, the team member will feel highly valued and, therefore, can continue to work better.

Once you have seen changes in the productivity of some workers, before taking disciplinary actions, consider the possibility of any mental issues behind the worker's problematic behaviour. Often, with workers experiencing a disruption in mental health, there occur changes in appearance, behaviour, and performance – missed deadlines, tardiness, repeated mistakes or interpersonal conflict. These are signs and symptoms of a mood disorder.

So before going down the route of disciplinary action, you share your observations and concerns with them. Of course, you cannot tell them of your suspicion of mental illness but your concern about the changes in their behaviour and performance at work. Point out concrete examples but positively present them – avoid blaming and being judgmental to encourage them to open up. Ask them how you can help. Also, explore with the person accommodations that may help them get back on their feet and running productively once again.

When mental health is concerned, it is vital to engage works in developing their solutions and enhance existing strengths. Here are tips on how to help them achieve these goals.

- Understand the worker perspective – the one having performance issues before discussing with them possible solutions.
- Instead of delving with what happened and who is responsible, focus on the solutions.
- Assist them in developing solutions instead of providing them.
- Before denying any request, try to understand underlying reasons for these requests as behaviours are attempts to meet their needs. While you may not be able to satisfy their requests, you can often satisfy the underlying needs.

TAKE TIME TO RELAX

Everyone needs a break from time to time, although many people find holiday a luxury that they leave their holiday time unused. But whether you take your leave or not, it is still essential to take a break from the daily routine, from the job, and from the demands of life to keep stress levels in check.

Taking a break doesn't mean procrastination or stepping away from responsibilities, but it is a way of taking care of your health so you can stay productive at work and in life.

Here are some of the many reasons why we need to take a break.

TO AVOID CHRONIC STRESS

It is normal to have the stress every day but allowing stress buildup can be unhealthy. Our body is designed to respond to short-term stress, but when stress is prolonged, and its symptoms are triggered repeatedly and regularly, the situation can quickly turn into a state of chronic stress.

People who previously experienced chronic stress are more prone to conditions including frequent headaches, gastrointestinal issues, hypertension, stroke, and heart disease. Once the level of tension in the body accumulates to a certain point, stress can quickly snowball because we are invariably in a state of reactivity.

At this level, even a positive situation can prove to be overwhelming if they require energy to enjoy, and you can't respond because of anxiety.

THE BENEFITS OF TAKING A BREAK

Enjoying a holiday or even short breaks can provide you with physical and psychological space from the constant demands of life. If we are in a relaxing environment, we feel less stressed. However, leave brings more than that. A holiday interrupts the cycle of stress that leads to us feeling overwhelmed. With a break from chronic stress, we can have physical and mental restoration. When a chronically-triggered stress response can cause a decrease in memory, creativity, and other mental functions, this break in the stress cycle can result in sharper thinking and increased creativity that can spill to all areas in life. With these, we can perform better at our jobs; have more time to enjoy with family, and live healthier and happier.

Sometimes, it's apparent that we need to take some leave, but most of the time, when stress sneaks up on us, we fail to recognise when we are at risk of burnout. Because each of us responds to stress in many ways, the signs may also differ. However, some general warnings may be recognisable in most cases. So if you spot any of the following symptoms, it's a good idea to start planning some downtime to recharge your mind and body.

PHYSICAL CUES THAT TELL YOU MUST TAKE A BREAK

- Change in sleeping pattern
- Feeling frustrated most of the time
- Lack of energy and vitality
- Mild health issues
- Lack of motivation
- Felling fuzzy-headed

It's always a good idea to manage stress to avoid getting overwhelmed. Regular self-care including that of your mental health plus breaks and holidays can keep you at your best.

If you need a break, there are many options from which you can choose. You can have a simple but relaxing break or long luxurious ones. You may even take a minute-long break to get you through the day so you can be more productive and keep yourself from getting overwhelmed, which you can hard-wire into your schedule.

Most workers may find working remotely not that easy to catch up with since they are used to going on-site or showing up in person so that they find themselves able to do their jobs efficiently. Because of what the whole world is going through nowadays, professionals like employees, freelancers, or managers are all forced to work online. Aside from them, remote workers are already working in the internet world. So, can you imagine that almost all workers are now pressed to do their duties via the internet?

You may find work at home, not your ideal way of working, especially if you are the outgoing type. Or you will find it hard to focus on your job if your home is now your office as well. Many other non-online workers share the same sentiments, but on the other hand, those who are working remotely effectively have already enjoyed the benefits of working from home. One of these benefits is that they enjoy working away from the pressure of their office.

Since most employees have just rushed into this new way of work, mostly unprepared, with no resources and lack of tools, it is understandable that you are not aware of the actual benefits of working remotely. The following steps will help you maintain a positive outlook about working remotely, whether you like working remotely or not. Your mental health should come first, so take time to think about your self-care strategies, before you get down to work. I hope this gives you a boost of positivity.

Social life doesn't end in social distance.

Social distancing may be the issue here so that you may feel frustrated or lonely most of the time. It doesn't mean that you will disconnect yourself from others even to those who are dear to you. If you think about the welfare of your loved ones and think about this situation as only temporary, you can look at the brighter side.

Through technology, you will still find yourself enjoying having free and open interactions, and sharing moments with your family and friends even though physical closeness is absent. People are finding ways to interact with their social groups through constant video chats instead of meeting up in coffee shops. You can also join virtual parties or board game nights. Some even use live streams for cooking food together.

Stay connected.

Try having phone calls or video chat with your family and friends to keep in touch with them as you drink coffee and relax at your home. If you the outgoing type, this is a convenient way and adds more opportunities to connect with people.

Staying connected with people you love is not difficult to achieve and just takes a little effort on your part. A daily dose of these two will keep your social life healthy. You can hear or see other people, offer help, empathise, or support each other with them as much as possible.

Organise a precise daily schedule.

Your office is now your home, but the problem is: since your home and work are in the same environment, you find yourself working more hours than when you are in the office outside the home. As funny as it sounds, this happens to remote workers unless they learn to divide their time for work and time for their life (this includes hobbies, family, and friends). Remote workers tend to find it difficult to separate from work since they already spent their whole day working at home.

Set your schedule and be precise about following it. It's beneficial if your company has fixed your 8-hour-schedule for you, then afterwards, you can focus on other things. If not, you can be more lenient with your time by dividing it into 4 hours in the morning and 4 hours in the afternoon or night.

You can schedule duties that need more creative juices or analytical skills in the morning. Then, work that requires repetition or administration can be set at night since you may have been exhausted already and less productive at the end of the day.

Most remote employees find scheduling helpful, and it gives them stability to work without crossing the boundaries of work and home. Otherwise, don't be surprised if you still find yourself working overtime without having any real breaks at all.

Set your travel itinerary.

If travelling is life for you, you will probably find giving it up equal to spending life in a mental asylum. But remember that life must go on and instead of lamenting on your cancelled trips, use your time indoors to prepare for your dream trips. It's the perfect time to make itineraries of places where you want to go. You don't have to buy tickets yet; you can find new places to include in your itinerary.

Visit online events.

No wonder most events are cancelled by their companies, but sure enough, these events such as educational or cultural activities can still be enjoyed by people like you.

Online conferences from other theatres around the globe and Paris Opera have free shows via the internet. You can also attend a LinkedIn live event, Twitter chat, or an online stand-up show.

. . .

Maintain physical fitness.

The forty-five minutes you lost every day when you're stuck in a city traffic jam before can be made use for staying fit now that you work remotely. Choose a type of exercise that will suit your taste and personality, and then make it a habit. There are many options, like stretching, yoga, or weight lifting.

You may find setting physical exercise as a routine helps you in dealing with stress and having your mind at peace. Also, exercise will boost your immunity as well as it can keep your body in good shape, improving your productivity, and helping you to unwind from things that give you negative thoughts.

No pressure for professional improvement.

Want to improve your skills to further your career prospects? While this may sound impossible when you are physically away from the office, you can find lots of resources that are just a few clicks away. You can read books about your profession or enrol in online courses without pressuring yourself about preparing for your next project or meeting up with your deadlines.

If you are the type of person that has difficulties in staying focused, you can ask other people with the same profession and struggles as you for guidance, tips, or advice on how to expand on your trade.

You can also write your thoughts or the advice that you got from other professionals in your blog, social media, or ebook. It may help you understand more about your work situation and garner more tips from different people that are willing to share and speak their minds. Then, you can learn and grow in your profession more.

Pursue new hobbies.

Since you have more time for yourself than staying in a traffic jam or spending time when you commute to work, why not pursue a hobby that you want before you started as a remote worker? It's time that you work on that hobby. It may be reading a book, studying new languages, learning how to play musical instruments or how to cook, listening to podcasts, or simply relaxing.

Duties first before distractions.

Get yourself a position in your home that you can call your designated workplace away from distractions that may come from your family. This place should allow you to continue uninterrupted while working, where no one is permitted during work hours and that you have to partake in no other activities except work whenever you are there. Take care of how your desk is organised by putting things that will make you feel relaxed and focused. You can also set an ambience that will make you feel comfortable and motivated to work in your workplace (e.g. lighting candles or playing music). If you find you are distracted by non-work thoughts, write them down on a list that place at the exit of your workspace then deal with them after work.

Take breaks.

Take time for yourself by taking breaks or calling your

friends or family. Watch videos or TV once in a while with your children without feeling guilty. It doesn't mean that you should not prioritise your work. It only means that you should consider your health, physical, or mental health it may be and don't push yourself too hard by overworking or multitasking. Concentrate on a specific task only and relax afterwards.

HEALTH BENEFITS OF TAKING A VACATION

Many studies proved that taking the time to get away from your job can have its physical and psychological health benefits. Those people who take regular vacations have lower levels of stress, a measured perspective of life, reduced risk of heart disease, and more inspired to achieve goals (Walden University, 2020). Here are more benefits of taking time away from work.

Improved Physical Health

Stress is a common culprit for many ailments, including heart disease and high blood pressure. According to a report of the New York Times, taking a vacation every two years rather than six years lowers risk for heart attack or heart disease (Tugend, 2008).

Improved Mental Health

A research study revealed that the human brain structure is altered by constant exposure to cortisol – the stress hormone, which is a contributing factor in anxiety and depression (R. Bernstein, 2020). Once away from work, you get relief from stress as calmness sets in, allowing the body and mind to heal in ways that aren't possible when under pressure.

Greater Well-Being

A Gallup Study cited that people who are always travelling got a 68.4 score as measured by Gallup-Healthway's Well-Being Index compared to a score of 51.4 for those who travel less frequently. The study found that there are improvements in the quality of sleep and mood three days after a trip. These health improvements remain throughout their holiday and even five weeks after especially to those who had more personal time and overall satisfaction during their vacation (Gallup, Inc., 2020a).

Heightened Mental Ability

Studies found that chronic stress can affect the processing and recall of memories. A high concentration of cortisol can cause declarative memory disorders ("The impact of stress on body function: A review," 2017, p. 1). Chronic stress can affect that part of the brain that inhibits goal-directed activity resulting in memory-related issues. Having some time off can help tune up your brain.

Improved Family Relationships

Spending some enjoyable moments with people you love can strengthen relationships. According to a study conducted by the Arizona Department of Health and

Human Services, women participants who took holidays were more satisfied with their marriages.

Decrease Burnout Risk

People who take time to relax regularly are less likely to end up suffering from burnout. They are also more creative and productive than their overworked counterparts who may rarely take time to rest and relax.

Boost Happiness

You can boost your happiness by merely planning a holiday, and according to a research study, this activity is the most significant boost. The effect of planning a trip could last for eight weeks before making the trip.

Simply put, by making an effort to remove stressors can improve many areas of life – health, relationships, job, perspectives, and self-motivation. It can likewise provide us with the break needed to recharge and rebalance our life for better handling of what is to come in the future.

DIFFERENT TYPES OF BREAKS

VACATION

Many people never realised how vital a holiday is, which is probably why they never make use of their leave days when they could have enjoyed them.

A holiday could mean out of town or out of the country travel that is restful and fun while you leave your work behind and not think of them. Work means stress, and it must be entirely out of your path while on vacation.

Because holiday time should mean total relaxation, do not overload your itinerary with activities that by the time you're through with your vacation, you feel you need another holiday to relieve yourself of the tiredness from your holiday activities.

STAYCATION

The staycation is becoming more in fashion nowadays when people have a greater need to take a break but could not afford an expensive international trip. Staycation merely is taking rest and relaxing at home. It is the same as a restful vacation – it means no domestic chores, office work, or any other regular responsibilities. You may turn off your devices – emails, social media channels, and make sure that you only rest, play, and enjoy yourself.

A staycation can be a better alternative to an expensive and well-planned trip as you can save both time and money. However, you need to have enough amounts of determination and self-discipline to be able to achieve what you hope for – which is RELAXATION.

Here are some strategies you can adopt to make sure that your staycation will indeed be a relaxing activity instead of an extension of your typical working day.

Turn off Your Devices

If your goal is to have a restful and relaxing vacation at home so you can take a break from the hustle and bustle of everyday affairs, make it a point to get away from the demands of your regular life. Since your devices are your closest link to your hectic schedule and pile of workload, you should turn them off. If you don't want to set yourself free from the world completely, set your phone to redirect callers to your voicemail. You can then check your messages and calls before bedtime and decide whether you want to return calls or respond to messages depending on the urgency of the need.

However, it may be a good idea to tell everyone that you are going to take a break for about a week and won't be answering any calls or messages. This little step will put your mind at ease and help you turn off anything related to work. You may tell them that you're going to a place where there is no access to the internet.

While being a remote worker makes it difficult for you to get away from work when you spend your staycation right where you work, it's best that you completely close that particular area (office space) in your home. It will be tempting to check on your work as your teammates are likely to request anything from you, which is the more reason why you need to get away from your computer and workplace.

Try Something Else

While on a staycation, you can have the opportunity to explore places in your hometown where you have never been before. Because you have been working all the time, you might have missed some new food or entertainment spots that have opened.

Visit them, and you will be amazed to see how your hometown has changed a lot and how you have missed all those changes while you locked up yourself in your virtual office every day.

When you have missed a lot of these experiences after you go back to work, you can revisit these places which can provide you with nice little escapes that are sure to help stave off burnout.

Avoid Overbooking!

While indulging in all the fun, remember that the idea of a staycation is for you to feel that you have a break, so don't overlook the fact that you also need more time for your body and mind to rest. Schedule some downtime when you can relax, sleep, read, play games with your family, or watch movies together. Spending time in the kitchen to learn some new recipes will also give you a pleasurable relaxation while being with your loved ones. The key here is to regain your balance back.

Don't Be Afraid to Spend

While you have been staying home too long while working remotely, you have saved more enough to spend this time on your staycation. Spend like you would do it while on holiday. You can go shopping, visit a spa, get a massage or pamper yourself.

After all, you've earned them. If you are living alone on your own, you may hire a cleaning service if you haven't used one yet without feeling guilty. All these will contribute to a carefree mindset which you must capture while on your full staycation. It's the splurging that will surely make the difference between a real staycation and a week of just hanging around your home.

PLAYCATION

Playcation is what other people call it when you just stay home and still manage to make it all fun! When staycation is focused more on relaxing and resting, PlayStation, on the other hand, is merely for the sake of fun.

After all the hard work and the monotony of daily routines that characterise the lifestyle of many remote workers, it is vital to inject fun into your life. You can do anything you enjoy while at home as a way to recharge yourself.

SHORT BREAKS

There are times when our body just needs to take a break from stress long enough to disrupt the body's stress response cycle. You may take a morning or afternoon walk to the park, ride your bike, or do a 10-minute meditation session just as Google and Apple encourage their employees to do. The Mindfulness technique, which is a breathing exercise is an excellent way to take a break while keeping your mind and body healthy even in your workplace.

MEDITATION FOR MANAGING STRESS

Who wouldn't want a few moments of peace and disengage from a hectic day for at least a couple of minutes if you think that you are taking in too much pressure?

Try to meditate whenever you are in an anxious, worried,

or tense state. Meditating for at least a few minutes is helpful so that you can restore your inner peace and state of calm. Meditation doesn't require any special tools or equipment, and you can meditate anywhere, at any time. The best part of it: Meditation is free and straightforward. You can meditate while you are walking, waiting for the doctor, riding a vehicle, or in the middle of a formidable business meeting.

Understanding Meditation

Thousands of years ago, Meditation is practised so that individuals could have a deep understanding of life's sacred and mystical forces. Nowadays, it is used to reduce stress and to help you maintain a relaxed condition. Still, Meditation is recognised as a medicine that compliments the mind and body.

When you are meditating, you eliminate stress by expelling the stream of jostling thoughts that fills up your mind through concentration, resulting in a deep state of tranquillity and relaxation of the mind.

Meditation Gain

Meditation is known for its numerous benefits. It can balance, tranquilise, and give you a sense of peace that may be beneficial for your overall health, including your emotional well-being. It also helps you manage medical condition-related symptoms and enables you to stay calm throughout the day.

Emotional Welfare With Meditation

Every day, your mind processes information. This acquired information tends to build up until a time comes that your mind becomes overloaded with information, and that contributes to stress. Through Meditation, your mind gets cleared from information overload and the resulting stress.

The following are what Meditation does for your emotional health:

- You gain a new point of view on stressful situations
- You can deal with stress easier and more confidently
- Your self-awareness increases
- You can focus on the present moment
- You can control your negative emotions
- Your creativity and imagination increases
- You can be more patient and tolerable

TYPES OF MEDITATION

Meditation is a broad word used for various practices that share the same result – a state of being relaxed or achieving inner peace.

Ways to meditate can include:

Guided Meditation

Also known as guided by visualisation or imagery, this meditation method can be practised by the leading of a teacher or guide. As you form mental pictures of situations or places that you find relaxing, you also try to use senses such as sight, smell, sound, and texture. The more, the better.

Mantra Meditation

This type of Meditation is performed by quietly repeating a calming word, phrase, or thought so that you can avoid thoughts that may distract you.

Mindfulness Meditation

This meditation type is based on your mindfulness - having an augmented acceptance and awareness of living in the present moment. Here, you practice broadening your conscious awareness as you focus on what you experience during Meditation (e.g. Breathing flow). You can observe your emotions or thoughts, but you also let them pass without judgment.

Qi Gong

It is a combination of relaxation, Meditation, breathing exercises, and physical movement practice to maintain and restore balance and considered a part of the traditional medicine of the Chinese culture.

Tai Chi

As a form of gentle Chinese martial arts, Tai Chi (pronounced as tie-chee) is practised by performing a self-paced series of movements or postures gracefully while exercising deep breathing.

Transcendental Meditation

This technique allows your body to stay relaxed in a profound rest state. You can be able to achieve inner peace effortlessly and even without concentration. Transcendental Meditation is a natural and straightforward technique wherein you repeat a personally assigned mantra silently. It can be a sound, word, or phrase that you repeat in a specific way.

Yoga

This ancient art promotes physical flexibility and mental tranquillity as you carry out controlled breathing and a series of postures. In yoga, you will be encouraged to lessen your concentration on your busy day. Poses that require focus and balance will move your thoughts more at the immediate moment.

MEDITATION ELEMENTS

Even if many types of Meditation differ from one another, they still vary in some features that will suit you, so that you can meditate more. These features vary according to the guide or teacher of your meditation class. The following listed below are some traditional features in Meditation:

Focused Attention

One of the essential elements of Meditation is the focus. You will need to concentrate on a specific image, object, a mantra, or your breathing. When you focus your attention, it helps your mind to be free from distractions that result in worry and stress.

Relaxed Breathing

The deep even-paced breathing of the diaphragm muscle is used to expand your lungs in practising this technique. It enables you to slow down your breathing by more oxygen intake and lessens the use of neck, shoulder, and upper chest muscles while you breathe. This technique will keep your breathing more efficient.

A Quiet Setting

It will be easier for you to meditate if you choose a quiet spot with fewer distractions – no radios, phone, or television. Eventually, you will be able to meditate anywhere, even in stressful situations where you need Meditation the most. You can meditate in a stressful work meeting, traffic jam or while queuing in a long line at the grocer's shop.

A Comfortable Position

As you aim to meditate, try to be comfortable and keep good posture. You can meditate while doing other activities or positions such as lying down, sitting, or walking.

Open Attitude

When thoughts begin to occupy your mind, just let it pass without judging it.

HOW TO PRACTICE MEDITATION DAILY

You may think that attending classes in specialised meditation centres or those led by trained instructors are the key to meditate correctly. You can still have quality meditation even if you have no one to teach you in person.

When you choose to practice Meditation on your own, you can make it formal or informal as long as it suits your situation or lifestyle. Though some people infuse their daily routines with an hour of Meditation, you can meditate even for a few minutes as long as you spend quality time meditating. Quality meditation is what matters.

Here are steps to learn so you can practice Meditation on your own at any time.

Step #1 – Breathe Deeply

Who doesn't know how to breathe deeply?

This meditation step is a good start for beginners because it is a natural body function. Concentrate on your breathing and make it your focal point as you listen and feel it. Breathe slowly and deeply as you inhale and exhale through your nostrils. Gently return your attention to your breathing whenever your focus wanders off.

Step # 2 – Scan Your Body

Try to focus on different body parts and be aware of its sensations. It could be tension, pain, relaxation, or warmth. When you merge breathing exercises with body scanning, visualise that you are breathing relaxation or hear in and out of those body parts.

. . .

Step #3 – Repeat a Mantra

Try to create your own secular or religious mantra. Sacred mantras are Jesus Prayer of Christianity, The Holy Name of God in Judaism, Om Mantra of Hinduism, or other spiritual mantras from Buddhism and eastern religions.

Step #4 – Walk and Meditate

Walk while you meditate is an efficient and healthy way of relaxation. Use this technique when you walk in a city sidewalk, mall, or a tranquil forest. When you practice this, instead of focusing on your destination, focus on your movements; walk slowly and deliberately. Focus on your leg or feet movements. Then, in your mind, repeat action words like lifting, moving, and placing while you lift your foot, step forward with your leg and place your foot on the ground.

Practice meditating and don't focus on judging your meditation skills. It may also contribute to additional stress if you keep doing so. Instead concentrate on your object of concentration, movement, or sensation. Your thoughts may eventually wander as you control your mind but remember to always return to your focal point.

There's no proper or improper way of Meditation. Just experiment and explore meditation techniques that you think will suit you at the moment. As long as it reduces stress and settles you into an overall good condition, you can enjoy the benefits of Meditation.

OTHER EXERCISES TO RELIEVE YOURSELF OF STRESS

Engage in Prayer

Prayer is an example of Meditation that is widely practised and most prominent. You can find it written or spoken in most faith traditions. Pray using your word or read written prayers by others. You can ask religious leaders such as priests, rabbis, or pastors for possible resources. You can also check your local library or bookstore's self-help section.

Read and Reflect

By reading and reflecting for a few moments on sacred texts or poems' meanings, many individuals report that they gained benefits. Listening to spoken words or sacred music (any kind of relaxing or inspiring music will do) can be beneficial. Then, write in your journal and discuss with your friend or spiritual leader, the reflections that you wrote.

Focus Your Love and Gratitude. This Meditation requires your attention to focus on a sacred being or image and fill your thoughts with feelings of gratitude, love, or compassion. Use your imagination as you close your eyes or look at your image representation.

PROVIDE REMOTE SOCIALISATION OPPORTUNITIES

Now that many are working at home, we are starting to realise that it's not all fun and games. Physical isolation and separation from each other pose enormous challenges for collaboration, as when you can't personally see the person you're working with, you can lose that sense of connection.

Without being together, working in the same room, it becomes harder to relate to one another. When you can't see facial expressions, gesture, body language, and other non-verbal cues, it's harder to connect, and an essential emotional context can be easily misinterpreted which could weaken relationships with teammates.

However, bonding is still part of a collaborative effort as you build effective teams on meaningful connections, trust, and inclusivity.

To break the monotony of working remotely, hanging out and connecting with teammates is still possible and should be actively encouraged.

For many people, their workplace is significant to their

social life. In a survey conducted with 1,000 employees, it found that friendships existing at work were considered more valuable to employees over a pay rise. It is more likely that employees are more engaged, productive, and happy when surrounded by meaningful relationships in their workplace. With the right tools in place, working remotely need not seem too remote after all. Here are some of the many ways to socialise remotely with your team and stay connected, human, and sane.

TURN ON VIDEO AND SCHEDULE CALLS

When working remotely, there is this good chance that you won't be interacting with anyone in person the whole day or even for days. Because it is crucial to maintain that human interaction when conversing with teammates, better opt for a video call, or at least a voice call when discussing project instead of text-based chatting. Hearing your co-worker's voice or laughter and seeing how they respond when you crack a joke in real-time can instantly bridge the distance.

TAKE VIRTUAL LUNCH BREAKS TOGETHER

Eating alone can be dull when working remotely. Schedule a lunch date with your teammates to keep up with those regular lunch chats.

You can all enjoy a meal together over a video conference call. Catching up with what you did over the weekend while eating meals together can be more fun when done virtually.

KEEP DINING AND DRINKING TOGETHER

It won't be much trouble remembering to keep in touch with your co-worker while stuck in your virtual space but less-regular catch-ups like occasional dining and drinking with them or bumping into each other at a coffee shop at more at risk of falling by the wayside as they are most likely to be impromptu events. An informatics professor at UC Irvine, Melissa Mazmania said that it might help to proactively schedule a date via video chat that serves as a sort of "What's going on with you these past few days?" to compensate for the lost interactions.

According to Heff Hancock, a communication professor at Stanford University, one reason why we want to hang out with someone is to strengthen the bond of friendship often through eating and drinking together. Through video chat, we can stimulate it.

Committing to a dinner or lunch with someone is a way of saying that you care for the relationship and that you want more than just an intermittent texting thread that each team member contributes to when they have the time. Besides, everyone needs to eat, even at the busiest of times.

CREATE TIME FOR CASUAL CHATS

Without the physical space for a usual hangout, your conversation with teammates could revolve around work alone. When everyone is apart, it's easy to overlook the morning small talks you usually have. Try starting your conversations with the usual generic chitchat before diving into the topic, although make sure not to dwell longer to affect your work. You can send your teammates some memes, funny stickers or videos to start everyone's day with a smile or share a cool song to listen to while working. These simple off-topic chats can go a long way in maintaining connections with your remote friends at work.

DUPLICATE SOCIAL NETWORKING FEATURES

Try searching for digital workplace tools that will enable you to create community forums, profiles, group chats, and virtual interactions that are usually present in commercial social networking platforms. Whether you used these to focus on work or work casually with these features, they are a great way to duplicate the interactive elements of an office via virtual means, therefore, making it easier and enjoyable than ever to maintain that sense of being in a community while apart from each other.

CELEBRATE MILESTONES WITH EVERYONE IN THE TEAM

Celebrating things like birthdays or work anniversaries does not have to be limited to the physical office space. You can strengthen team connection via a screen monitor by retaining a culture of recognition and positivity. Customised stickers can be a great tool to easily acknowledge someone's a major milestone in work or life and make them feel recognised and appreciated in a personal and fun way.

OFFER ENCOURAGEMENT AND SHOW YOUR SUPPORT TO OTHERS

Managers need to acknowledge that stress is present even more so in a remote setting. It is essential to listen to team members' anxieties and concerns while empathising with their struggles. It is more important, especially for new members of the remote team who is still in need of making some adjustments on their own. If it becomes clear that a team member is struggling but not communication stress or anxiety, it is your place to ask how they're doing. Asking them how a remote work situation works for them can elicit valuable information that you might not otherwise hear if you hadn't asked. Make sure that you are willing to listen carefully to what your team member has to say once you ask. To be sure that you understand them clearly, restate it briefly. Focus on the stress and concern of your team member rather than on your own.

According to Julianne Holt-Lunstad, a Psychology professor at Brigham Young University, a critical element of feeling socially connected is by receiving support from others or even just knowing that they are there to call on when needed. Research also indicated that offering support could be more beneficial to the one offering it than to the one receiving it.

Support can be provided in a variety of forms. It can be a physical act such as offering to drop off extra food if needed, or it may be through information as a response to a friend seeking some advice. It can also be emotional – checking in to see how a friend is weathering it all. Just knowing that support is around the corner can dampen stress responses.

Research studies about emotional intelligence and how to contain anxiety tell us that employees are looking to their team managers for cues on how to react to crises situations or some sudden changes. If you, as their manager, communicated across your team, stress, and helplessness or show signs of being hopeless, it will trickle-down to your remote team members (Barsade, 2002, p. 644) (Harvard Business Review & Brewer, 2020).

Effective remote leaders usually use the two-pronged approach which acknowledges the stress and anxiety that any of the team members might be feeling in a difficult situation, but at the same time, they likewise provide affirmation of their confidence on the individual by saying, "I know this is quite tough, but I believe that you can handle it!"

With you supporting them, employees are more likely to take up the challenge.

HOLD REMOTE COMPETITIONS

Light competitions are fantastic mechanisms for team building. You may find a lot of remote team building activities on the internet. You can learn about each member's culture by sharing recipes, music, dances, and many more.

SET UP VIRTUAL WELL-BEING CLASSES

When you don't have the physical buffer between work and private time because you're working at home, so make sure that you watch over your well-being as well as that of your remote team workers. There are many ways that you can load fun and excitement into group activities. You may consider setting up a yoga class every week. Apply this idea to all areas of healthy living to give your workers the chance to relax, chat, share news, and videos.

FINAL WORDS

Working with a remote team or teams is a great responsibility for a remote manager. It can be challenging to manage a group of individuals coming from different locations, time zones, cultures, and personalities. However, if run well, it can be beneficial not only to the company, especially if you happen to be the owner but to yourself and the people in your direct line.

Adapt yourself to look after yourself. Look at your diet and treat your food as medicine. Learn to recognise the signs of mental health decline. Adapt your working environment to remove distractions and improve your chances of remaining productive. Take breaks and plan them into your documented structured day. Add in some regular exercise. Just as in an emergency in an aeroplane, you should put on your own oxygen mask first, only if you look after yourself first will you be in a position to be able to handle the problems of your team members.

Remote work is now becoming the career trend of the century, and if you can master the skill of effectively managing a productive remote team, it could mean success for your business or your career prospects as a remote manager.

Now that we have come to the end of the book, we hope you have gathered enough information and resources to master the craft. However, learning is not enough without applying it. As you apply it, continue learning to refine the skills outlined here. After all, education is a continuing process.

Knowledge is essential in every aspect of life, may it be in your personal, family, business, career, or relationships with other people and applying what you have learned from this book in all areas of your life will lead you to success and life-work balance.

Let's stay in touch! Visit me at https://nearlydone.press/erwtfm/ to sign up for my mailing list and get extra insights not found in this book.

RESOURCES

Analytics, G. W. (2016, March 1). Costs and Benefits. Retrieved July 30, 2020, from https://globalworkplaceanalytics.com/resources/costs-benefits

Barsade, S. G. (2002). The Ripple Effect: Emotional Contagion and Its Influence on Group Behavior. *Administrative Science Quarterly*, 47(4), 644. https://doi.org/10.2307/3094912

Bernstein, P. (2013, November 5). SearchYourCloud Survey, It Takes up to 8 Attempts to Find an Accurate Search Result. Retrieved July 30, 2020, from https://www.techzone360.com/topics/techzone/articles/2013/11/05/359192-searchyourcloud-survey-it-takes-up-8-attempts-find.htm

Bernstein, R. (2020, June 9). The Mind and Mental Health: How Stress Affects the Brain. Retrieved July 30, 2020, from https://www.tuw.edu/health/how-stress-affects-the-brain/

Billable Hours for Professional Services - Replicon Case Study. (n.d.). Retrieved July 30, 2020, from https://www.replicon.com/case-study/fisher-vista/

Bloom, N. (2014, August 21). To Raise Productivity, Let More Employees Work from Home. Retrieved July 30, 2020, from https://hbr.org/2014/01/to-raise-productivity-let-more-employees-work-from-home

Buffer. (n.d.). State of Remote Work 2020. Retrieved July 30, 2020, from https://lp.buffer.com/state-of-remote-work-2020

Cues of working together fuel intrinsic motivation. (2014, July 1). Retrieved July 30, 2020, from https://www.sciencedirect.com/science/article/abs/pii/S0022103114000420

Gallup, Inc. (2019, December 12). Re-Engineering Performance Management. Retrieved July 30, 2020, from https://www.gallup.com/workplace/238064/re-engineering-performance-management.aspx

Gallup, Inc. (2020a, January 5). Taking Regular Vacations May Help Boost Americans' Well-Being. Retrieved July 30, 2020, from https://news.gallup.com/poll/180335/taking-regular-vacations-may-help-boost-americans.aspx

Gallup, Inc. (2020b, June 18). Majority of U.S. Employees Not Engaged Despite Gains in 2014. Retrieved July 30, 2020, from https://news.gallup.com/poll/181289/majority-employees-not-engaged-despite-gains-2014.aspx

Harvard Business Review, & Brewer, J. (2020, April 16). Anxiety Is Contagious. Here's How to Contain It. Retrieved July 30, 2020, from https://hbr.org/2020/03/anxiety-is-contagious-heres-how-to-contain-it

IDC Forecasts U.S. Mobile Worker Population to Surpass 105 Million by 2020. (2015, June 23). Retrieved July 30, 2020, from https://www.businesswire.com/news/home/20150623005073/en/IDC-Forecasts-U.S.-Mobile-Worker-Population-Surpass

Indeed. (2018, December 14). REPORT: Remote Work Brings Benefits, but Attitudes Are Divided. Retrieved July 30, 2020, from https://www.indeed.com/lead/remote-work-survey

Kross, E., Verduyn, P., Demiralp, E., Park, J., Lee, D. S., Lin, N., ... Ybarra, O. (2013). Facebook Use Predicts Declines in Subjective Well-Being in Young Adults. *PLoS ONE*, *8*(8), e69841. https://doi.org/10.1371/journal.pone.0069841

Kuligowski, K. (2019, May 7). Distracted Workers Are Costing You Money. Retrieved July 30, 2020, from https://www.businessnewsdaily.com/267-distracted-workforce-costs-businesses-billions.html

Neuroscience News. (2016, February 24). Poor Short Term Memory Linked to Inability to Ignore Distractions. Retrieved July 30, 2020, from https://neurosciencenews.com/working-visual-memory-distraction-3726/

Nevogt, D. (2018, March 5). What is Employee Monitoring? Retrieved July 30, 2020, from https://hubstaff.com/employee_monitoring

Pantic, I. (2012, March 24). Association between online social networking and depression in high school students: behavioral physiology viewpoint. Retrieved July 31, 2020, from https://pubmed.ncbi.nlm.nih.gov/22447092/

Peek, S. (2018, December 27). Communication Technology and Inclusion Will Shape the Future of Remote Work. Retrieved July 30, 2020, from https://www.businessnewsdaily.com/8156-future-of-remote-work.html

Radiological Society of North America, Seo, H., & Jeong, E. (2017, November 30). Smartphone addiction creates imbalance in brain. Retrieved July 31, 2020, from https://www.eurekalert.org/pub_releases/2017-11/rson-sac111717.php

RehabChicago. (2020, July 30). The Human Brain. Retrieved July 30, 2020, from http://www.rehabchicago.org/the-human-brain/

Replicon. (2000). *Fisher Vista, LLC Realizes 85% Gain in Workplace Productivity with Replicon TimeBill*. Author. Retrieved from https://www.replicon.com/wp-content/uploads/2016/06/CaseStudy_fishervista.pdf

Schwartz, C. (n.d.). New Research: How Leading with Equality and Values Impacts Your Business. Retrieved July 30, 2020, from https://www.salesforce.com/blog/2017/07/impact-of-equality-business-research.html

Simovic, D. (2020, January 13). The Ultimate List Of Remote Work Statistics - 2020 Edition. Retrieved July 30, 2020, from https://www.smallbizgenius.net/by-the-numbers/remote-work-statistics/#gref

Stanford. (2006, May 21). Feeling the beat: Symposium explores the therapeutic effects of rhythmic music. Retrieved July 30, 2020, from https://news.stanford.edu/news/2006/may31/brainwave-053106.html

Strategy Analytics. (2016, November 9). The Global Mobile Workforce is Set to Increase to 1.87 Billion People in 2022, Accounting for 42.5% of the Global Workforce. Retrieved July 30, 2020, from https://www.strategyanalytics.com/strategy-analytics/news/strategy-analytics-press-releases/strategy-analytics-press-release/2016/11/09/the-global-mobile-workforce-is-set-to-increase-to-1.87-billion-people-in-2022-accounting-for-42.5-of-the-global-workforce#.WtQT1y7wbX4

The impact of stress on body function: A review. (2017). *EXLI Journal*, *1*(1), 1. https://doi.org/10.17179/excli2017-480

The Washington Post, & Fung, B. (2014, September 13). Study: Cities with super fast Internet speeds are more productive. Retrieved July 30, 2020, from https://www.washingtonpost.com/news/the-switch/wp/2014/09/18/study-cities-with-super-fast-internet-speeds-are-more-productive/

To Raise Productivity, Let More Employees Work from Home. (2014, August 21). Retrieved July 30, 2020, from https://hbr.org/2014/01/to-raise-productivity-let-more-employees-work-from-home

Toluna Group. (2018, February). *Udemy in Depth: 2018 Workplace Distraction Report* (1). Udemy for Business. Retrieved from https://research.udemy.com/wp-content/uploads/2018/03/FINAL-Udemy_2018_Workplace_Distraction_Report.pdf

Tugend, A. (2008, June 8). Take a vacation, for your health's sake. Retrieved July 30, 2020, from https://www.nytimes.com/2008/06/08/business/worldbusiness/08iht-07shortcuts.13547623.html

Walden University. (2020, April 1). 5 Mental Benefits of Exercise | Walden University. Retrieved July 30, 2020, from https://www.waldenu.edu/online-bachelors-programs/bs-in-psychology/resource/five-mental-benefits-of-exercise

Printed in Poland
by Amazon Fulfillment
Poland Sp. z o.o., Wrocław